P9-CRA-601

home book of
# SMOKE-COOKING
## COOKING
### Meat,
### Fish
### & Game

# home book of SMOKE-COOKING

## Meat, Fish & Game

Jack Sleight &
Raymond Hull

with sketches by Jack Sleight

**STACKPOLE BOOKS**

HOME BOOK OF SMOKE-COOKING MEAT, FISH & GAME

Copyright © 1971 by STACKPOLE BOOKS
Published by
STACKPOLE BOOKS
5067 Ritter Road
Mechanicsburg, PA 17055

First printing, September 1971
Second printing, April 1972
Third printing, July 1972
Fourth printing, January 1973
Fifth printing, May 1973
Sixth printing, April 1974
Seventh printing, October 1974
Eighth printing, April 1975
Ninth printing, December 1975
Tenth printing, May 1976
Eleventh printing, August 1976
Twelfth printing, May 1977
Thirteenth printing, January 1979
Fourteenth printing, December 1979
Fifteenth printing, May 1980
Sixteenth printing, October 1981
Seventeenth printing, (*paperback*), July, 1982
Eighteenth printing, (*paperback*), December 1982
Nineteenth printing, (*paperback*), June 1983
Twentieth printing, (*paperback*), November 1983
Twenty-first printing, (*paperback*), November 1984
Twenty-second printing, (*paperback*), June 1985
Twenty-third printing, (*paperback*), April 1986
Twenty-fourth printing, (*paperback*), April 1987
Twenty-fifth printing, (*paperback*), May 1988

ISBN 0-8117-2195-7
Library of Congress Catalog Card Number 76-162445
Printed in the U.S.A.

# Contents

HOMEMADE SMOKE OVENS
Wheelbarrow • Box • Branches • Plywood: Folding Model • Shed • Refrigerator • Stove • Barrel • Barrel and Box • Masonry • Cement Blocks
COMMERCIALLY-MADE SMOKE OVENS
Portable Metal • Portable Ceramic • Built-in Metal
OTHER EQUIPMENT
Cutting Equipment • Brining Containers • Oil • Non-stick Spray • Brushes • Scales • Thermometers • Extra Racks • Gloves • Sausage Equipment • Refrigerator
FUEL
Hardwoods • Which Hardwood? • Preparing the Wood • Charcoal • Starting A Fire

SALT
Flavoring • Dehydration • Preservation • Improved Appearance • Purchasing Salt • Storing Salt • The Strength of Brine • Measuring Salt
WATER
OTHER INGREDIENTS
CORRECT USE OF BRINES
Containers • Immersion • Overhauling • Temperature • Time • After Brining
BASIC FISH BRINE
BRINE FOR OCTOPUS OR SQUID (INK FISH)
DRY CURE FOR FISH
SPICED DRY CURE FOR FISH
SWEET PICKLE BRINE FOR MEAT
THE BRINE PUMP
Filling the Pump • Injecting the Brine • Quantities • Cleaning the Pump
DRY CURE FOR MEAT
BASIC SEASONING
SEASONING FOR CURED MEATS
SMOKED SALT

NO-SMOKE ROASTING
OVEN TEMPERATURES
A USEFUL PRECAUTION
HOW MUCH IS ENOUGH?
BASTING
STORAGE OF SMOKED MEATS

PLAIN SMOKED MEATS
>Beef, Lamb, Pork Roasts • Steaks • Pork Chops or Spareribs • Spareribs and Sauerkraut • Meat Balls, Meat Loaf • Hearts • Hamburgers • Ground Beef • Cold Meats, Sausages, Etc.

CURED SMOKED MEATS
>Beef Ribs • Corned Beef • Rolled Roast • Cured Tongue • Cured Hearts • Peruvian Cured Hearts • Kidneys • Jerky • Jerky: Quick Method • Smoked Cured Beef • Sleight's Special Beef Sandwich

DRY CURING
>Quantities • Application • Modifications

BACON AND HAM
>Strong Cure Bacon • Old-style Ham

CHICKEN
>Splitting • Seasoning • Smoking • Use of Ordinary Oven • Serving and Storage • Reheating

SMOKED TURKEY
>Seasoning • Smoking • Use of Ordinary Oven • Serving and Storage

SMOKED DUCK AND GOOSE
>Plucking • Hot Smoking Process • Cold Smoking Process • Serving and Storage

GAME BIRDS
>Preparation • Seasoning, Serving, Etc.

BRINE-CURING POULTRY AND GAME BIRDS
>Procedure • Special Marinated Chicken Wings

SMOKED LIVERS, HEARTS, GIZZARDS
>Scalding • Seasoning • Smoking • Oiling • Cured Hearts, Gizzards • Marinated Livers, Hearts, Gizzards

SPECIAL DISHES WITH SMOKED LIVER
>Smoked Liver Stuffed Eggs • Smoked Liver Paste • Smoked Paté De Foie Gras

IN THE FIELD
>Promptness, Cleanliness • Smoking

CURED SMOKED VENISON
>Fat Content • Dry Curing • Serving • Modifying Recipes

SMALL GAME ANIMALS
JERKY
HEARTS
TONGUES

BREAKFAST SAUSAGE
    Ingredients, Grinding and Seasoning • Stuffing and Smoking • Storing
    and Serving • Other Notes
SPECIAL SAUSAGE SANDWICH

SMOKED CHEESE
SMOKED NUTS
SMOKED SEEDS
SMOKED EGGS
SMOKED FROG'S LEGS
SMOKED BLUEBERRIES
GARLIC BREAD

CANNING TECHNIQUES
    Sterilization • Liquid Contents • Testing

EQUIPMENT
    Smoke Oven • Refrigeration • Other Equipment
MATERIALS
RECORDS
ECONOMY
MENU PLANNING
MARKETING

# CHAPTER 1

# The Art
# of Smoking Food

THERE HAS LATELY OCCURRED a powerful upsurge of interest in traditional arts and crafts. Many people are no longer content to work at one specialized occupation and to buy from others all the products and services they need; they find a keen satisfaction in making and doing things for themselves. Home-grown flowers and vegetables, furniture built, skins tanned and mounted in one's own workshop—such things give a double pleasure, in the making and in the using.

The art of smoke cookery and smoke curing seemed, a few years ago, to be nearly extinct. Big-scale commercial smoking was being supplanted by new methods of food preservation; some so-called "smoked" foods were prepared without any real application of smoke. Few city-dwellers knew or cared that it was possible to smoke food at home; the few who wanted to try found that published information was scanty, and some of that unreliable.

But the situation is changing. Smoke-ovens of various designs are being manufactured and sold in large numbers; hardwood for smoke generation is easily available; magazines and cook-books are beginning to print a few smoked-food recipes and instructions.

Now this book offers a thorough instruction course in the art of smoke cookery and smoke curing. Whether the reader decides to buy his apparatus or to make it, whether he undertakes to prepare a few hors d'oeuvres for two people or a smoked-food banquet for two hundred, whether he wants to smoke a moose quarter, a sockeye salmon, two pounds of meatballs or two dozen oysters, this book will show him the way.

## THE JOYS OF SMOKE COOKERY AND SMOKE CURING

What can one expect to gain in return for the time and effort invested in smoke cooking and curing?

### Conservation

We are becoming increasingly aware of our duty to avoid waste, whether of food or any other resources. This book describes quick, simple techniques by which a fisherman may conserve his catch in the field, and be sure of bringing it home in good condition for eating pleasure! Moreover, smoke curing does not simply preserve food, but heightens and improves its flavor; it yields a finished product that actually tastes better than fresh-cooked meat, fish or game!

### Economy

Many commercially smoked foods are expensive. Typical prices recently observed are:

Sliced smoked turkey, 3 ozs. for 69¢ = $3.15 per lb.
Sliced party salami, 4 ozs. for $1.09 = $4.36 per lb.
Canned smoked clams, 3⅔ ozs. for $1.33 = $5.81 per lb.
Sliced smoked salmon, 3⅔ ozs. for $2.79 = $12.91 per lb.
Canned smoked salmon, 3¾ ozs. for $1.65 = $7.04 per lb.
Packaged smoked beef, 2½ ozs. for $1.10 = $7.04 per lb.

Jerky, 1⅞ ozs. for $1.79 = $15.36 per lb.

Smoked foods can be made at home much more cheaply than they can be bought in stores.

## Fine Flavor

The quality called "flavor" is a composite sensation, resulting from the combined effects of taste, smell, touch and sight.

There are four basic tastes: salty, sweet, sour and bitter. All the complex tastes we know are various combinations of these.

The importance of food odors is not generally recognized although it is a common experience that food seems flavorless when one's sense of smell is dulled by a head cold. The sense of smell is vastly more powerful than that of taste; some people can distinguish ten thousand different smells. It is specially through this sense that smoked food makes its distinctive appeal.

Different foods appeal by their textures to the sense of touch of the lips, tongue and inside of the mouth.

Visual appeal also contributes to the total flavor effect; food is less flavorsome if eaten in the dark. Smoked foods have a variety of rich, attractive colors.

Controlled smoking processes, then, can favorably influence the taste, smell, odor, texture and appearance of food, and so produce a wide variety of flavors that cannot be attained by ordinary cooking methods.

Good flavor heightens the diner's enjoyment of food, and aids digestion. This benefit is obtained, to a much greater degree, with home-smoked rather than with commercially-smoked foods. The commercial food processor must necessarily cater to an assumed average customer; but home-smoked food can be prepared exactly to the cook's own taste!

## Personal Satisfaction

There is a keen pleasure in offering to family and friends better smoked food than they can buy in any store. Even more satisfying is it to produce smoked delicacies that cannot be bought in the food store, at any price. That is true of many foods described in this book.

Moreover, after some experience with the methods and recipes given here, one can proceed to develop original recipes and modified methods that will yield absolutely exclusive food products! It is possible to sell home-smoked food, and so develop what began as a hobby into an enjoyable and lucrative part-time or full-time business.

## HISTORY OF SMOKE COOKERY AND SMOKE CURING

The earliest method of food preservation was drying. Cereals, fruits, meat and fish can be preserved at least from one harvest to the next and, under favorable conditions, much longer, if thoroughly dried and kept dry.

In the Neolithic age, men learned to use smoking as a preservative technique. Smudge fires were built under drying-racks so that the rising smoke would keep flies away from the meat and fish, or so that the gentle warmth would speed the drying process. Thus the stone-age people found that smoke somehow made the food keep longer than plain sun-dried food, and that smoke improved the flavor of the preserved foods.

At a later period, the application of salt, dry or in brine, was introduced as a preliminary to smoking. This technique—known as "curing"—improved the flavor of smoked foods, and extended their potential storage period.

Salt was readily available by solar evaporation of sea water to people living near the sea in hot climates. In colder countries and at places far from the sea, salt was a precious rarity, and some people used instead potash (potassium carbonate), obtained from wood ashes, as a curing agent.

Until recently, in historical terms, smoking served almost entirely as a *preservative* process. Meat and fish were given a high salt content—up to 15%—and were subjected to days or weeks of cold-smoking (below 85° F.) during which the food was dried and flavored, but not cooked. Thus treated and then kept dry, meat and fish will keep indefinitely, with no sign of decay, even at summer temperatures.

This kind of preserved food was necessary for domestic use when transportation was slow, when mechanical refrigerators were unknown and when natural ice was in warm weather an article of luxury, obtainable only by the wealthy. Such food was also used to supply armies on long campaigns and to feed the crews of sailing ships on voyages that might last two or three years.

This hard-smoked meat and fish was far too salty, far too tough, to serve as a ready-to-eat food; it required a lengthy soaking to remove some of the salt, and then cooking to make it palatable.

The 19th century and early 20th century saw the development of fast steamships, of railroads, mechanical refrigeration, and abundant supplies of artificially-made ice. Meat and fish could now be held for long periods in bulk cold storage, expeditiously transported far from their point of origin, and kept safely for days or weeks in the home.

These technical changes have reduced the demand for heavily smoked and salted meat and fish to the point where very little of such products is used in industrialized countries, although there is still some demand for them elsewhere.

Thus the emphasis shifted away from smoking as a system of preservation, towards smoking as a means of enhancing the flavor of foodstuffs and as a system of cookery. Commercial smoking establishments increased their production of lightly-salted (2% to 3%) meat and fish, hot-smoked for no more than a few hours at temperatures between 85° and 250°F., and ready to be eaten without any further preparation, or with nothing more than warming in pan or oven.

This is the aspect of food smoking that will be principally described here; most of the foods are meant to be eaten soon after they come from the smoke oven or, if kept at all, to be kept fairly briefly under refrigeration.

There will, however, be some recipes for foods that can be kept with or without refrigeration for a long time.

## THE SMOKING PROCESS

As a matter of interest, and as a means of obtaining full control over apparatus and ingredients, it is desirable to know something of the way in which smoke acts upon foodstuffs which are exposed to it.

### Composition of Smoke

Most people think of smoke as the gray or blue-gray cloud that rises from a fire. That cloud consists of microscopic droplets of various chemicals formed by burning wood. But, mixed with the visible smoke is an invisible cloud of hot vapor; that vapor plays an important part in food processing.

The major flavoring components of wood smoke are aldehydes,

ketones, carboxyl acids and phenols. These chemical components are mixed with, and carried aloft by, a column of hot air which also plays its part in the total smoking process.

## Effects of Smoke on Protein Foods

The action of smoke on foods is complex and not yet fully understood; but here is a simplified account of the processes involved:

The hot air partially dries the food and renders it less susceptible to decay. Moreover, because of this removal of water, the food becomes a somewhat more concentrated source of nutriment than the same food unsmoked.

Chemicals from the smoke condense on the food. Some of them remain at the surface, where they help to produce the characteristic smoked-food coloration.

Other chemicals dissolve in the liquid content of the food. (Fresh meat and fish contain substantial amounts of water, usually from 40% to 80%.) Thus dissolved, the smoke ingredients can penetrate below the surface and carry the smoke flavor deep into the center of the food.

In addition to flavoring the food, these chemicals kill, or check the multiplication of yeasts, molds and bacteria, microorganisms which are the principal causes of decay. This powerfully aids the preservative action already begun by the drying process. Salt also has a strong bactericidal action; this effect is discussed in Chapter 3.

Fats and oils in fresh foodstuffs, when exposed to air, tend to combine with oxygen and turn rancid. The phenols in smoke function as antioxidants and prevent this form of deterioration.

## A WARNING

Much has been said about the powerful flavor-building and preservative action of smoke. Nevertheless, smoking is no magic process that will restore freshness and good flavor to food that is already deteriorating; it is a waste of time and materials to process tainted meat or fish! The little extra care required to bring food to the brining bath and the smoke oven perfectly fresh and perfectly clean will be abundantly repaid by heightened flavor and improved keeping quality for the finished meat, fish or game.

## RECORD KEEPING

Trichinosis can be controlled in three different ways: thorough cooking; freezing of the raw meat for a minimum of 21 days; or, after making it into sausage, allowing it to cure with the seasonings and curing agents for a minimum of 21 days.

Meat, fish and game are not uniform, standardized products like chocolate bars or sugar cubes; they vary markedly from time to time and from place to place. Different fish—even of the same species—contain different amounts of fat or oil; they may vary, in oil content and in other ways, from one part of the year to another. Butcher's meat and game meat will vary markedly according to the age and condition of the animal from which it was taken.

Different smoke ovens—particularly if they are homemade—will produce and distribute smoke differently, and will have different temperature zones in different positions within the smoke chamber. Different fuels to supply heat, different kinds of wood used for generating smoke, all these introduce additional variables.

The distraction caused by a phone call or an unexpected visitor may result in a piece of meat lying longer than usual in the brine bath prior to smoking, or remaining longer than usual in the smoke oven. The shortage of one seasoning ingredient may lead to substitution of another.

It requires only a notebook and pen to keep simple records of each batch of smoked food. Note such things as:

Type of food. If relevant, note the weight or size, the source from which it was obtained, and the date.

Brief record of the brining, dry-salting or seasoning processes used, including any experimental ingredients, and the *time* of brining or salting.

Details of smoking—time, temperature, type of wood used for smoke, color and texture obtained.

Any further processing after smoking.

A final assessment of the results obtained—too salty, not salty enough, just right for salt, oversmoked, undersmoked, rather tough, deliciously tender, etc.

Then, six months later, when it is necessary to smoke another fish of the same species and size, another similar piece of butcher's meat, or another similar game animal, the notes will be a valuable guide to the elimination of any slight errors, and to the repetition of former successes. By these simple means, a beginner in the art of smoke cookery and curing can quickly attain the status of an expert, and can learn to produce mouth-watering smoked foods *every time*.

# CHAPTER 2

# Equipment for Home Smoking

THIS CHAPTER DESCRIBES SEVERAL different kinds of smoke ovens. Note the word "oven." Home smoked-food makers sometimes speak of the "smoke box" or "smoke house." Yet many of the recipes in this book call for some degree of heat; for best results the apparatus should provide not only a supply of smoke, but also a controlled temperature range. So "oven" is the more accurate term.

Smoke ovens may vary in complexity from a plain cardboard box to a large steel, thermostatically-controlled, insulated oven. They may vary in cost from nothing at all up to several hundred dollars. They vary widely in size; one person, preparing smoked food for himself, will need less oven capacity than another who is smoking food for a large family and a number of guests. Size will be determined, too, by the kind of product that is treated. Fair quantities of smoked clams, oysters, chicken livers and such small items can be smoked in one cubic foot; but to smoke yard-long sausages or joints of moose meat requires much greater capacity.

## BASIC ELEMENTS

There are five requirements for an efficient smoke oven. Each is discussed under a subhead below. The first four are essential; the last is desirable.

### A Source of Smoke

This can be:

A slow-burning, smoky hardwood fire.

A charcoal or briquet fire topped with hardwood chips or sawdust so that it produces smoke. The fire can be lighted in a bucket with holes punched in it, in a metal pan, in a hibachi, or any convenient container.

An electric heating element on which stands a metal pan containing the hardwood chips or sawdust. A hotplate with a control giving two or more ranges of heat is especially useful.

A natural gas or butane gas burner heating the pan of hardwood chips or sawdust.

The smoke source should always be placed at the bottom of the oven.

### An Area to Confine the Smoke

The smoke oven may be simply a cardboard or wooden box, or a tent-like enclosure of canvas or plastic, although those materials obviously will not stand much heat. A tent of metal foil erected over a small smoke source such as a hibachi would serve quite well. An old refrigerator, icebox, stove, chicken house, toolshed or child's playhouse can be adapted as a smoke oven. One can build or buy specially made ovens of brick, stone, concrete, aluminum, iron, steel or pottery.

## Racks or Hooks

The meat or fish must be hung up or laid out so that the smoke can reach every part of its surface. Most whole fish and such meats as sausages and hams will hang safely. Twisted paper-clips, by the way, make good small S-hooks. But fish fillets and small, tender fish such as smelt are not strong enough to be hung up; they will fall apart as they cook. Food laid horizontally on racks gets smoked uniformly if it is turned over half-way through, assuming that an efficient baffle is fitted to disperse the smoke uniformly. Food that hangs from hooks probably will be smoked a little more thoroughly at the bottom than at the top.

## A Draft

The smoke must be kept moving from the bottom to the top of the oven so that it continually passes over, heats and imparts flavor to the food. In one of the loosely-built temporary arrangements here mentioned, there will probably be enough air escapement to make an adequate draft. But a permanent, well-built smoke oven needs a controllable air inlet at or near the source of smoke, and also one or more controllable air outlets at the top.

Note that the top smoke outlet is absolutely essential! If smoke is confined in too great a concentration and allowed to stagnate about the food racks, it will impart an objectionable, sooty flavor to the meat or fish.

Adjustable bottom and top draft holes also give some measure of control over oven temperature. Yet, with no more control than this, the smoke would tend to gush straight through, rising in a narrow column from the smoke source towards the outlet, missing half the meat, and wasting much of its flavor potential on the chimney and outside air. So it is best to install one or more baffles; these baffles disperse the smoke into every corner of the oven, over every piece of food, and make it give up most of its heat and flavor before escaping.

## A Supplementary Source of Heat

This *extra* heat source is in addition to the burner or heater that produces the smoke. Some of the designs which will shortly be described do not have this feature; the main heat source is hot enough to make the smoke and cook the food, too. That is, except, perhaps, for poultry or roasts that need high heat. But for big smoke ovens, and for some kinds of food, the extra heat source is highly desirable. It permits, for example, the production of meats that are thoroughly cooked, yet only lightly smoked. Many people like food this way. This would be achieved by putting less hardwood on the fire or heat source.

The supplementary heat source saves time, too, in bringing the oven up to working temperature.

A three-speed or a two-burner electric hotplate is useful for this purpose. So is a one or two-burner gas or butane hotplate.

## HOMEMADE SMOKE OVENS

Here are some of the materials and designs that can be used to make temporary or permanent smoke ovens.

### Wheelbarrow

In a metal wheelbarrow put a layer of sand or vermiculite, enough so that, when leveled out, it will be about six inches thick. A six-inch layer of small rocks is a good alternative; it lets air through to make a natural draft.

Support a metal oven grate or some similar grid about a foot above the bed of sand with bricks or tall cans at the four corners.

Under the grate kindle a fire of charcoal. When it is burning, put the hardwood smoking material on top.

Lay the meat or fish that is to be smoked on the grate, covering it with heavy-duty aluminum foil. Do not wrap the foil entirely around the food. Bend it into a rough dome shape to trap the smoke and heat. Leave it open at the bottom, and with a nail punch a few holes in the top of the "dome" to make a draft to draw the smoke around and over the food.

Operating Notes:

Turning the barrow in relation to the wind will to some extent control the heat and smoke produced by the fire.

To control the fire in a strong wind, build a little wall of bricks, rocks, or pieces of sheet metal that will partly shield the charcoal from the wind.

Remove the foil cover from time to time, turn the food over if it is cooking too fast on the underside, and watch it closely to see when it is done.

## Box

A cardboard, wood or metal box will make a serviceable temporary smoke oven for use in the back yard or on a hunting expedition in the bush, to conserve fresh-taken fish or meat.

Dig a firepit about two feet square and two feet deep. From the firepit dig a trench about nine inches deep and wide, running *downwind* from the pit. The length of the trench depends on the material of the box. Cardboard will stand less heat than wood, wood less than metal. For cardboard, the trench should be at least three feet long; for wood, two feet; for metal, one foot.

To prepare the box, punch small holes in the sides and run sticks or wire through; on these hang or lay the fish or meat. Punch one or two holes in the top of the box for smoke vents; movable rocks or bits of wood will serve to vary the size of these openings and so control smoke flow and internal temperature.

Place the box over the end of the trench. Cover the top of the trench with boards, metal foil, or branches and dirt, to transform it into a tunnel.

Between the firepit and the tunnel, contrive a damper from a sheet of metal to control the flow of smoke and hot air into the tunnel.

Light a small smoky hardwood fire in the pit, and partly cover the pit so that the wind forces smoke along the tunnel and through the box.

Operating Notes:

Note that the longer the tunnel, the cooler is the smoke by the time it reaches the box, and the longer it will take to semi-cure meat or fish.

Some people like to expose their fish or meat for 10, 12 or more hours to cold smoke (i.e. smoke at the same temperature as the outside air). There is, in fact, no particular merit in that procedure; 90° to 100° of heat will accomplish just as much in four or five hours, with absolutely no impairment of flavor.

## Branches

A hunter or camper far from home with not even a cardboard box to spare, can still smoke meat successfully.

Cut six or eight Y-shaped branches and half as many straight ones. Stick the Y's in the ground and lay the straight sticks horizontally on the crotches.

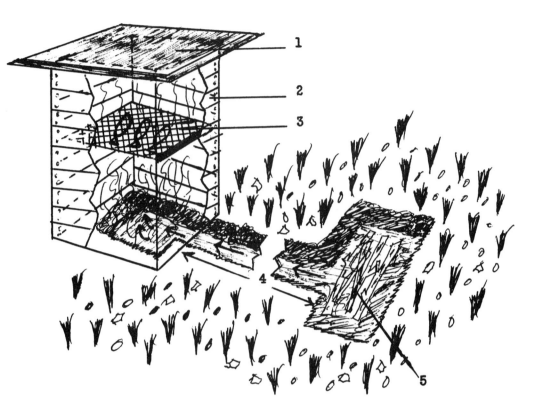

**Box Smoker**

1—Plywood or sheet-metal cover. Raise edge for draft or use holes in the cover.

2—Something to confine smoke:
- a. Cardboard box
- b. Wood box
- c. Old refrigerator
- d. Barrel

3—Screen or rack for fish or meat. There are alternates:
- a. Rods thru side of smoker
- b. Hooks from cover

4—Ditch in ground to lead smoke into smoker. Must be covered and may vary from 2′ to 10′ in length.

5—Fire Pit—partially covered to direct smoke thru tunnel.

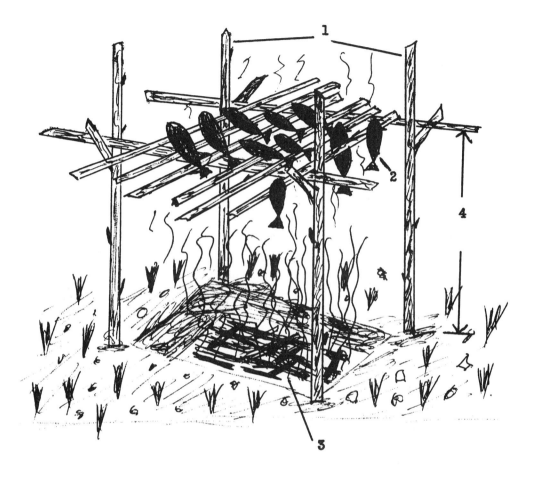

1—Uprights. Cut 12″ above branch that holds crosspieces. This is to hold canvas, blanket, etc., cover above fish.
2—Lay or hang fish on crossbars.
3—Firepit underneath, or use tunnel method.
4—Variable height—minimum 18″.

Hang the fish or meat from the horizontal sticks.

Cover the whole structure with boughs, canvas, sheet plastic, or any other available material that will confine the smoke.

Operating Notes:

If the air is motionless, cut the Y sticks long so that the fish hang three feet off the ground; then build a small smoky hardwood fire right underneath.

If there is a breeze, cut the sticks shorter, so that the fish hang near the ground; use the firepit and tunnel method described under "Box" to guide the smoke from the fire to the fish.

## Plywood: Folding Model

A good portable smoke oven can be made of plywood, to fold flat for convenient storage in a boat, camper or trailer.

A hotplate is the most convenient heat source for this model, but there are several alternative ways to provide the requisite smoke and heat in locations where electricity is not available. On the beach, a small fire ring could be made with rocks; fire can be kindled in a large empty can with some holes punched in its sides. Next to electricity, the most convenient heat source would be a hibachi.

Here are some hints on construction.

Shape and Size.     The most convenient form is a rectangular box about two-and-a-half times as high as it is wide. For example, a box 18″ × 18″ × 42″ would be appropriate for use with a 12-inch hibachi. In any case, the sides of the oven must be well clear of the fire container, and there should be a two foot clearance between the hibachi and the top of the oven.

Materials.     To avoid warping under the influence of heat and weather, the plywood should be at least 3/8″ thick. Marine plywood would be very good, but a less costly outdoor grade will suffice.

The specific measurements given here are for the mentioned 18″ × 18″ × 42″ oven. There should be no difficulty, however, in adapting them to make larger or small models.

The back and the two sides are the same size, 18″ × 42″. On the side panels, nail horizontal wooden cleats 1″ × 1″ at 18″, 24″, 30″ and 36″ from the bottom. When the oven is set up, the upper three pairs of cleats support wire screen racks, 18″ × 18″ on which the

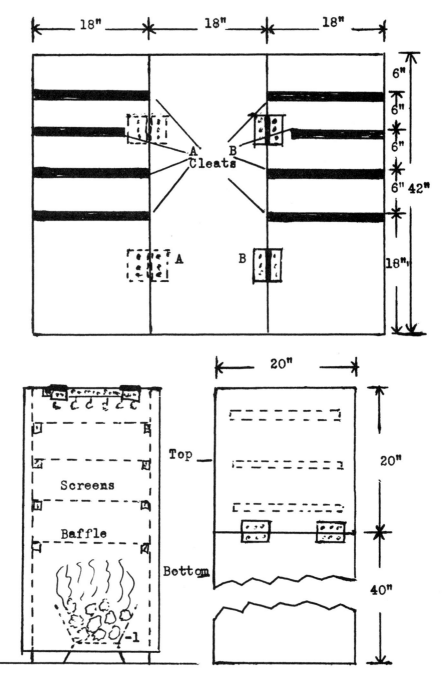

**Plywood or Sheet-Metal Portable Smoke Oven**

Hinges marked "B" should have removable pin, otherwise, because of cleats, may not fold flat. Hinges marked "A" are on outside, "B" hinges are on the inside.

1—Heat source—Hibachi, electric hot plate, butane burner, etc.

food is laid to be smoked; the lowest pair of cleats supports a sheet-metal smoke baffle, pierced with a number of holes.

These three pieces are hinged together so that they will fold flat for transport or storage.

The front panel is 20" × 40". The 2" extra width allow handholds for panel insertion and removal when the oven is assembled. When this panel is in proper position, its 40" height leaves a 2" gap at the bottom through which air enters to keep the fire and smoke going.

A simple way of supporting the front panel in position is to drill four small holes near its edges. These holes allow resting the panel over finishing nails set so as to protrude half an inch from the front ends of the top and bottom sets of cleats.

The top is 20" × 20". It has three 1" × 1" × 18" cleats nailed crosswise to its underside. Hooks can be screwed into these cleats if it is desired to hang up fish for smoking. The screw-hooks can be removed, if necessary, to save space when the oven is dismantled for storage.

Anyone with suitable tools and experience could build a similar portable smoke oven using sheet metal instead of plywood.

Operating Notes:

When using this smoke oven on a boat, put some old newspapers, a piece of canvas, or a piece of sheet plastic under it so that drippings of grease do not soil the deck.

If too much smoke leaks out between the joints, throw a piece of canvas or an old blanket right over the oven.

When smoking chicken, spareribs or other foods that may drip considerable amounts of grease, it would be a good precaution to place over the fire a tent-like cover of heavy aluminum foil, perforated with holes to let the smoke through. This will keep drippings from falling into the fire, causing undesirable flare-ups. This can be done with most any smoke oven where the fire is directly under the food.

Food-smoking on a boat (with this or any smoke oven) is bound to present certain problems through shortage of space and the motion of the boat so it is strongly recommended that before the smoke oven is taken aboard, it should be set up and used several times on land so that the operator becomes thoroughly familiar with its operation under safe, easy working conditions.

An unused shed of almost any shape or size can be adapted as a smoke house. One man in Seattle uses an old tool-shed about 8 feet by 10. He simply hangs the fish from the rafters, builds a slow alder fire in the middle of the dirt floor, and closes the door.

Here are some hints on converting or building a shed for smoking.

Building a fire on the floor is messy and inefficient. To save trouble, and to use fuel more economically, make a firebox. It may be a low wall of unmortared bricks arranged with some air spaces in the bottom row; it may be a five-gallon drum with some holes punched in it, or an ordinary barbecue. Such a firebox gives better control over heat and smoke production than can be achieved with an open fire. Over the firebox arrange a horizontal metal baffle to stop the smoke from rising in a narrow stream straight up to the roof.

To support meat and fish near the top of the shed, install a number of 2″ × 4″ joists and hang the food from them by metal hooks. An alternative is to build wooden frames that support removable metal stove-racks or sheets of heavy steel mesh. Do not, however, nail the metal racks into place. They must be removable for cleaning.

A controllable vent at the top of the shed is useful, unless the shed already leaks smoke in several places. Probably enough air leaks in under the door and elsewhere, to eliminate the need for building a special air intake at the bottom.

An electric hotplate may be used as heat source and smoke generator, but it should be grounded. Run a wire from the plate to a rod stuck in the ground.

Almost any kind of wooden enclosure will serve the purpose—an unused child's playhouse, a big dog kennel, a large packing case, etc.

If no such structure is available, it is not hard to build one. Lumber yards carry plans and lumber lists for sheds of various kinds. For such a walk-in model, it is best to give oneself plenty of room to move inside. Cut a vent hole near the roof, with a movable cover to vary its aperture.

Anyone who is unhandy at carpenter work can easily enough

erect one of the small prefabricated metal tool sheds now on the market. If this shed needs calking to prevent undue loss of smoke, stuff fiberglass insulation into the cracks.

*Caution!* While there will not likely be any very heavy volume of smoke emerging from the top of any of these referred-to small sheds while operations are in progress, always keep in mind that someone seeing smoke and unaware of the operations could possibly think an unattended shed on fire, taking steps to call the fire department. Be wary of this and, if anything, be perhaps less secretive respecting the character of the operations rather than details of the recipes.

## Refrigerator

A good smoke oven can be made from an old refrigerator. It is well insulated and so will hold heat, save fuel, and finish off food more quickly, for example, than the shed-type smoke house. The refrigerator already has a number of removable metal racks. It has a full-length door that is convenient for loading and unloading. Here are some hints for conversion.

It is best to keep the smoke-making equipment outside the storage compartment. This permits maximum use of the inside capacity for the meat or fish being smoked. Cut a hole about 8″ diameter in the floor; one inch above it, mount a horizontal metal plate as a baffle, to dissipate the smoke.

If the refrigerator is of the type that has the machinery underneath the storage compartment, remove the motor and compressor. Utilize this space for making smoke with a hotplate and a pan of hardwood chips. If the bottom section is a removable vegetable bin, do the same. Or, for maximum capacity, raise the refrigerator on four concrete blocks, cut a hole in the bottom, and set the smoke apparatus outside. Build an enclosure of plywood, metal or concrete blocks around the smoke source, so that the smoke cannot drift aside, but is forced into the refrigerator.

In the top of the refrigerator cut one 3″ or two 2″ holes. Arrange something—pivoted metal flaps, bricks, etc.—to control the aperture of these vents. Alternatively, fit a two-foot length of stovepipe with a butterfly damper.

Operating Notes:
To avoid cutting large holes, removing compressors, or making other major alterations, the hotplate and pan

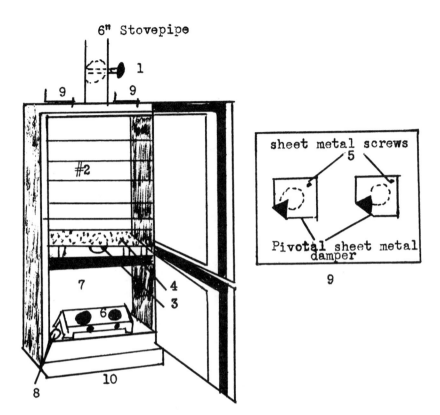

**Refrigerator Conversion**

1—Damper control
2—Shelves or racks
3—Smoke inlet hole
4—Metal baffle supported at 3″ to 4″ above smoking inlet perforated with many holes
5—Sheet-metal screws
6—Heat source:
    Electric hotplate
    Hibachi
    Butane gas burner
7—Old frozen food compartment, or refrigeration unit space
8—2 or 3—2″ or 4″ holes for draft
9—Alternate draft control
10—If refrigerator has no lower compartment, heat source may be placed right in the refrigerator, but preferably raise the refrigerator and build a lower compartment for the heat source.

of chips may be placed in the main storage compartment.

It is well to bear in mind that a refrigerator is *not* designed to withstand heat! The author once converted a 'fridge by cutting a hole in the bottom, then lit a fire of charcoal briquets underneath, using green boughs to make smoke. Around the edge of the hole, the insulation was exposed. All at once, the refrigerator caught fire and the insulation burned up! Several similar incidents have been reported. So, for safety's sake, use no other heat source than a hotplate inside a 'fridge. With an outside heat source, do not let flames come near the insulation. Whatever smoke generating system is used, beware of excessive heat.

To use the cold-smoke process, dig a firepit as described for the box-smoker, and lead the smoke into the refrigerator from a distance.

## Stove

An old electric cookstove can be made into a smoke oven in much the same way as the old refrigerator, although it will have a smaller capacity. It will be necessary to cut holes at the bottom and top of the oven to create a smoke circulation. As with the refrigerator, a hotplate and pan of hardwood chips would make a convenient smoke source.

The cookstove has two important advantages over the refrigerator. First, it will withstand a lot of heat. Second, if the original heating elements are retained, use of the thermostat or range heat control gives a well-regulated source of supplementary heat (i.e., in addition to the smoke source) that facilitates medium and high-temperature smoke cookery.

## Barrel

A simple, yet highly effective smoke oven can be made from an old steel oil or alcohol barrel of about 40 or 50 gallons capacity.

With a sharp cold chisel or a cutting torch, cut out the top of the barrel.

Trim the cut-out top to make it about 3″ less in diameter. Drill a dozen one-inch holes through this disk (more holes if they are smaller). The disk will now serve as a baffle. The holes let some smoke and heat through, while the rest rises around the edge of the disk.

The baffle is supported about half-way down the barrel. Here are four supporting methods:

Drill four holes in the side of the barrel; through these put *long stove-bolts* with about 3″ of each bolt projecting inside, and the nuts screwed up tight to the barrel side. The baffle will rest on the stems of the bolts.

Drill holes in the barrel and put two *iron rods through from side to side.*

Weld two *iron rods across the barrel.*

Make four *right-angle brackets* out of iron strip; weld or bolt them to the side of the barrel.

However this mounting is contrived, the baffle should be easily removable.

With chisel or torch, cut a firebox door about 8″ × 10″ in the side of the barrel, right at the bottom. If it is not right at the bottom, the remaining lip hinders cleaning ashes and soot from the barrel. The door should be hinged in place and fitted with a fastener to keep it closed.

From heavy steel screen, make two circular racks about 1″ less in diameter than the barrel. The bottom rack should have four upright columns or standards, about 8″ long, to support the upper rack. These standards also serve as handles for easy insertion and removal. The top rack is fitted with two drawer-pulls, or handles made of heavy wire, for insertion and removal. The handles must be strong; they must bear the weight not only of the rack but of the load of meat and fish that is on it.

Take a sheet of metal or plywood big enough to cover the top of the barrel. Cut one or two vent holes in this cover, with some simple arrangement to vary their aperture as required.

Operating Notes:

The lower rack must not rest directly on the baffle. Put four empty cans or four half-bricks on the baffle, so that the rack is supported 4″ to 6″ above the baffle.

For smoke, use an electric hotplate and a tray of wood chips. A natural gas or butane burner will be just as effective and in a steel barrel will create no fire hazard. A fire of charcoal or briquets will serve the purpose, covered with short hardwood boughs for making smoke.

Slightly opening the bottom firedoor and varying the

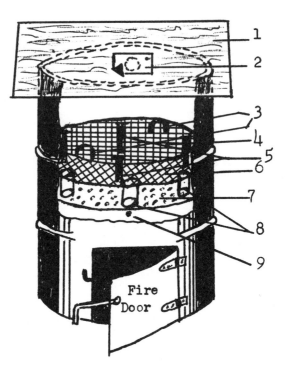

1—Plywood or sheet-metal top
2—Movable vent
3—Handles on top rack or screen
4—Top screen or rack
5—Upright supports on lower screen or rack 6″ - 8″
6—Lower screen or rack
7—Perforated baffle from end of barrel
8—Supports for lower screen—6″ - 8″ cans with ends removed
9—Support for baffle—at least 4 needed

aperture of the vents on top gives excellent control of the draft, and provides a useful range of temperature and smoke intensity.

To smoke smaller amounts of food or to operate in less space, make this smoker on a smaller scale by using a 25-gallon, 10-gallon, or even a 5-gallon barrel.

### Barrel and Box

This smoke oven is built from a steel barrel, any size that is available, and a wooden or metal box. The box can, if necessary, be built from scrap lumber, exterior or marine plywood.

In the top of the barrel cut a circular hole about half the diameter of the barrel.

Make a firebox door, size about 8″ × 10″, right at the bottom of the barrel, using chisel or torch as earlier described.

In the bottom of the box, cut a circular hole the same size as that in the top of the barrel.

From plywood or sheet metal, make a baffle, one inch less in length and width than the bottom of the box. Drill a number of 1″ holes at random in the baffle. Mount it on rocks or small cans about 2″ above the bottom of the box.

On the sides of the box next fasten 1″ × 1″ cleats to support the racks, which should be made of heavy steel screen.

In the top of the box, fasten hooks from which food such as fish may be hung for smoking.

Arrange that the whole front of the box opens on hinges or lifts off, for easy loading and unloading.

Cut two 2″ vent holes in the top of the box, with some suitable arrangement to vary their aperture, thereby controlling temperature and smoke density inside the oven.

Operating Notes:

> If smoke leaks out too fast from a loosely-constructed box, throw a piece of canvas right over the box to help confine the smoke.

### Masonry

Anyone capable of working with bricks and mortar, or with concrete, can build an excellent permanent outdoor smoke oven.

The simplest type would be a reproduction in brick of the refrigerator-smoker described earlier—a tall brick box with a smoke-generator at the bottom; next, a baffle to distribute the smoke; above that, several removable metal racks to hold the fish and meat and, on top, a brick or metal chimney with a damper to control the outflow of smoke and hot air.

There should be a door in front of the racks for easy loading and unloading. For this, the oven door from an old cookstove would do. For the bottom door giving access to the smoke-generator, the

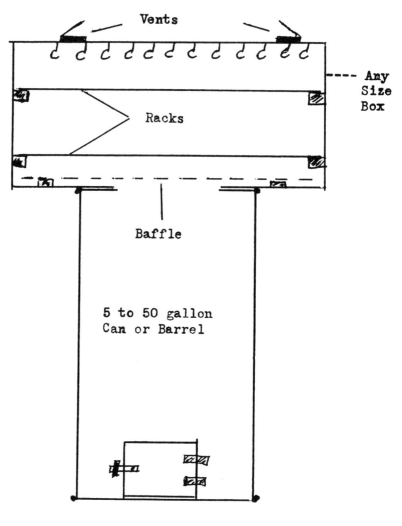

**Barrel and Box Smoke Oven**

firedoor from an old wood-and-coal stove with its built-in draft regulator would be ideal.

To support the racks, embed metal strips between the bricks on opposite sides of the oven. Alternatively, every other course can have two bricks projecting inward from the wall on each side of the oven.

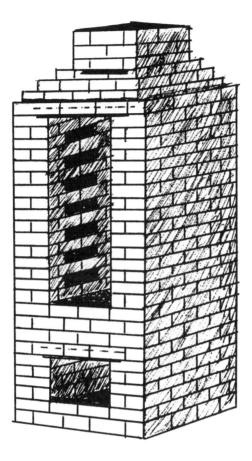

**Plain Masonry Smoke Oven**

Follow directions as given under Elaborate Smoke Oven and Barbecue, Chapter 2, for doors, damper, draft, etc.

Any masonry smoke oven, of course, needs a solid foundation because of its great weight.

A more elaborate structure is this combined smoke oven, barbecue, grill and storage area, designed and built by the author.

This one contained about 1,800 ordinary bricks, and 40 firebricks to line the firebox. The oven was designed to use stand-

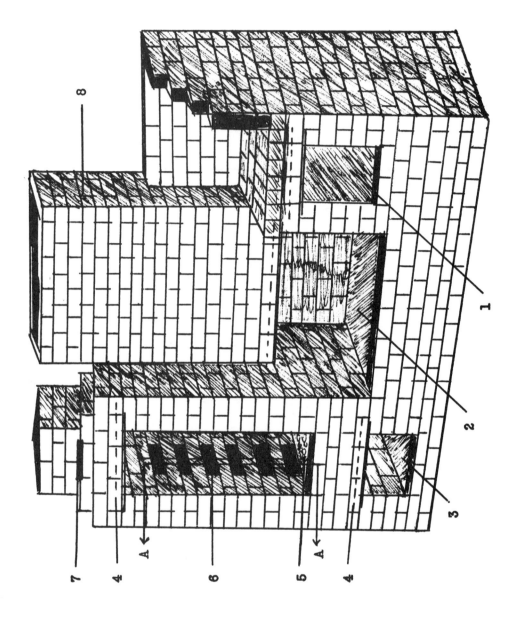

## Elaborate Smoke Oven and Barbecue

1—Storage area with work space above. Cover bricks, supported by plywood. Use metal or wood door. (If plywood is used in either instance, use exterior or marine type.) Have 2″ slope toward front for drainage.

2—Space for barbecue. Build width and depth to fit expected unit. Many different sizes and models are available.

3—Firebox lined with fire brick. Use metal door with sliding draft control.

4—Above each door and under front of chimney, support bricks with a sturdy angle-iron resting on side bricks, flange up in the back.

5—Install perforated metal baffle. If possible have two baffles, both removable.

6—Smoke oven compartment. Use a heavy iron door or door from a refrigerator. Build opening to fit your door if necessary. When refrigerator doors are used, remove rubber gasket, then place a coating of asbestos furnace cement around edge of opening to make air-tight seal. Use this sealing method for metal door, also. If compartment is made approximately 18″ wide, most ordinary domestic oven racks will fit.

7—Heavy sheet-metal sliding damper, installed while mortar is still damp and moved frequently until mortar sets.

8—Chimney for barbecue—have bottom 18″ above top of barbecue.

Walls on each side of all doors should be double brick thickness to embed hinges and door closures, but be sure to bend these rods so they will not turn or pull out.

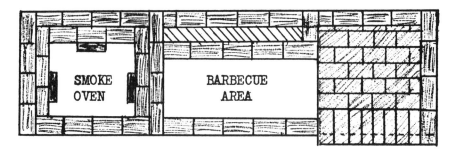

**Plan For Elaborate Masonry Smoke Oven and Barbecue**

Upper portion of chimney over smoke oven not shown—taper to suit size of oven chamber and dimension of bricks used.

Cross-section of smoke oven wall showing every other center brick extending into smoke oven chamber to hold racks for food. Strips of metal may be embedded as an alternative method. Both sides and rear of chamber are made the same.

ard oven racks. Many of the construction details are similar to those described above for the plain smoke oven, but here are some additional points:

Where the top is tapered to form a chimney, insert a piece of metal the size of the opening to form a sliding damper. Put it in while the mortar is soft, and move it frequently until the mortar sets.

When hinge-holders for doors are set in the brickwork, the part embedded in the mortar should be bent into a crooked shape. Then it will not turn and pull out.

Between the firebox and the oven is the kind of baffle described previously—a heavy perforated metal plate. Even better results would be obtained with two such baffles, 2″ to 3″ apart, with the holes staggered. Such arrangement would ensure the all-important even dispersal of smoke throughout the oven.

The performance of many a smoke oven, by the way, will be improved by insertion of an extra baffle. Hold the two baffles apart by bolts, by short metal cans open at both ends, or any other convenient spacers.

## Cement Blocks

A semi-permanent smoke oven can easily be made of standard 8″ × 8″ × 16″ cement blocks. On a level, firm foundation, no mortar is needed.

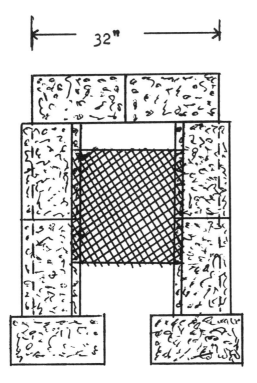

**Cement Block (8″ x 8″ x 16″) Smoke Oven**

Plan does not include top level. Top blocks are spaced so that racks or screens are readily removable to facilitate taking out smoked foods.

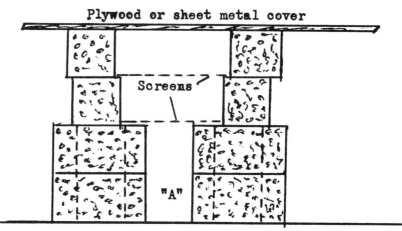

**Elevation**

Opening "A" may be adjusted by moving blocks.

Because of the large area of the firebox and the ample escapement opening between the blocks, no baffle will be needed with this design.

After the racks are loaded, a tarpaulin or a piece of old blanket should be draped over the front of the top part, to keep the smoke in.

The oven in the diagram needs 28 blocks. Bigger ones could be built by using more blocks. The width or length of the oven can be varied according to the size of the racks or wire screens that are available.

A similar smoke oven could be built of unmortared bricks, but it would not be nearly so sturdy.

## COMMERCIALLY-MADE SMOKE OVENS

Some people have neither the time nor the desire to build a smoke oven at home. For them, several kinds of ready-made smoke ovens are available at supermarkets, hardware and sporting-goods stores, and through mail-order catalogues. These ovens, if handled properly, will do first-class smoking.

## Portable Metal

A typical portable metal smoke oven weighs about 15 pounds. It has a rectangular aluminum case about 2 ft. × 1 ft. × 1 ft., and a steel inner lining to the actual oven portion. There is an electric heating element at the bottom on which rests a metal pan to contain the hardwood chips. The smoke rises past the meat, laid out on metal racks, and passes out of a controllable vent in the lid.

This type of smoker is operated exactly like the homemade refrigerator or stove-types previously described. It would be adequate for a few people but, with its working capacity held to little more than one cubic foot, it would not produce enough smoked foods for a big family or party.

Its great advantage is its easy portability. This smoker can be used indoors as well as out. Stand it in a fireplace, and its surplus smoke will drift up the chimney. An apartment-dweller with no fireplace can place it on top of a cookstove and turn on an exhaust fan to draw away the smoke. Meanwhile the other burners of the stove are available for cooking the rest of the dinner.

## Portable Ceramic

The Kamado or Japanese smoke oven is becoming popular nowadays, although it is generally advertised and used as a barbecue. Many Kamados were brought back from Japan by returning Servicemen and tourists. Now they are on sale here in import stores and other retail outlets.

The Kamado is made of ceramic, usually colored green or red. It looks something like a huge egg, with its smaller end flattened to make it stand upright, with a controllable smoke vent on the big end, and a controllable draft door in one side near the bottom.

The top third of the "egg" lifts up on hinges like a lid. With the lid open, the Kamado serves as grill or barbecue; closed down, the lid forms an oven for roasting or smoking.

At the bottom of the Kamado is a ceramic firebox with an iron grate designed to contain a charcoal fire. On the firebox sits a spacer ring, which supports a grill a few inches above the fire. For straight barbecuing, use charcoal alone in the firebox. For smoking, put hardwood chips on the charcoal fire.

Kamados come in several sizes, from 15″ to 31″ in height, and from 9″ to 17″ in grill diameter. Weights vary from about 25 lbs.

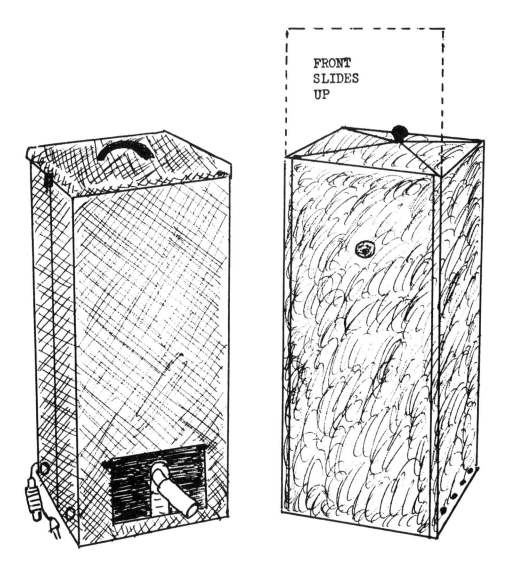

**Common Portable Electric Smokers**

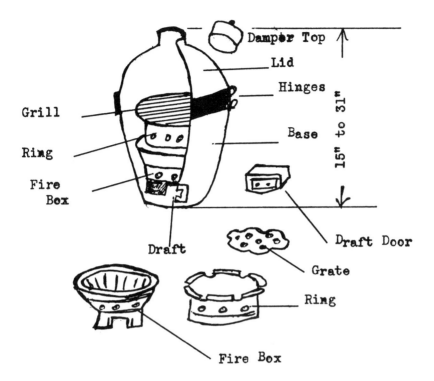

A different top draft and lower draft-door are available, made of metal to facilitate the regulation of the draft.

for the smallest models to about 150 lbs. for the big ones. Most users of the bigger sizes find they need wheeled trolleys to move them around. The latter are usually sold at the same stores as the Kamados.

There is a ceramic Chinese smoke oven, similar in operation to the Kamado, but barrel-shaped instead of egg-shaped.

Metal versions of the Kamado are now available. They operate on exactly the same principle. The smoke is enclosed in metal instead of earthenware. The metal oven weighs less than the heavy ceramic, but does not hold the heat so well.

Operating Notes:

Basically, the Kamado operates in the same way as the steel barrel smoker, but there are a few special points worth mentioning.

Some people have trouble starting the charcoal fire.

Helpful hints on that subject appear near the end of this chapter.

When the fire is started, its rate of burning and consequent production of heat and smoke, can be controlled—with practice—by adjusting the draft door at the bottom and the damper at the top. Naturally, the more air passing through, the faster the fire will burn; then, as the drafts are closed, the heat will accumulate inside. A useful practice is to stand an oven thermometer on the grill and stick a meat thermometer into the roast or whatever is cooking, to indicate when it is done. It is worth taking a little time to practice controlling the drafts, noting the effect on the oven thermometer. Once this skill is mastered, it is possible to maintain a very even heat in the Kamado, because its thick ceramic walls and lid hold heat so well.

*Warning!* The Kamado can be cracked by rough treatment, or by overheating it with too big a fire and all drafts closed. It may also crack if rain falls on it or if liquid is spilled on it while it is hot.

Most imported Kamados are porous, and so will absorb moisture if left standing outside. Then, although they appear dry on the surface, they may crack when heated.

There is a Kamado produced in the U.S.A. with a glazed finish, which withstands water and heat better than the porous ones.

There is one inconvenience with the Kamado: to add more charcoal or more hardwood for smoking, the user must lift out both the grill and the meat or fish on it, to get at the firebox.

## Built-in Metal

In the author's home is an excellent built-in metal oven, bought second-hand from a restaurant. No similar models are available ready-made, but a good sheet-metal shop could build one for about $400.00.

It is 40" high, 20" wide and 21" from front to back. The sides and top are of steel, well insulated to retain heat. It is designed to take movable metal racks 18" × 18".

In the box projecting from the bottom front is a small electric el-

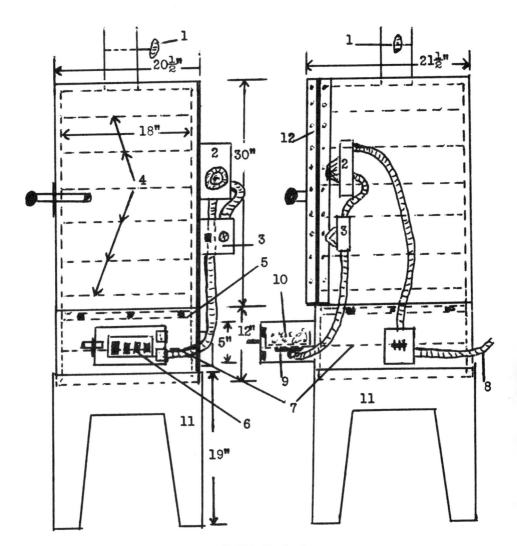

**Built-in Smoke Oven**

1—Damper in minimum 4″ pipe
2—Thermostat 0°—250°
3—Switch with red warning light
4—Screens or racks—removable
5—Double baffle; many holes—removable
6—Sliding draft-door
7—Heat element
8—220 volt electrical connection
9—Heat element for smoke
10—Pan for chips and sawdust
11—Base—a separate unit
12—Piano hinge

Capacity—up to 50 pounds. (3 12-pound turkeys, 2 17-pound hams, 45-50 pounds split fryers, 20 pounds shrimp).

ement on which the pan of hardwood sits to provide the smoke. The door of this smoke-box contains an adjustable damper. The oven is vented into the furnace flue, with a damper in the pipe to regulate the outflow of hot air and smoke.

Just above the smoke inlet and below the racks is a baffle, a piece of sheet-metal a little smaller than the interior dimensions of the oven, and pierced with many holes. This causes even distribution of the smoke.

Around the bottom of the main oven compartment is an electric oven element controlled by a thermostat. This permits reliable control of the oven temperature, and gives dependable results for smoking all kinds of food—small fish, big fish, chicken, turkey, jerky, or a smoked cured roast of wild game.

## OTHER EQUIPMENT

In addition to the smoke oven, some other items of equipment will be needed for easy, successful food-smoking. Much of it will already be at hand in the kitchen, or elsewhere in the home.

| | |
|---|---|
| Cleaver | Slicing knife |
| Boning knife | Meat saw |
| Steak knife | Knife sharpener and steel |

### Cutting Equipment

It is needlessly difficult—dangerous, too—to try cutting up meat or fish with a bread-knife on the kitchen counter. The safe, easy way is to use a solid cutting board or block, and proper meat or fish knives. Wherever necessary, the following instructions for meat, fish and game will indicate what tools should be used, but here is a list of the basic cutting equipment:

### Brining Containers

Some kind of vessel is needed to hold the brine while meat or fish are being soaked in preparation for smoking.

For a few oysters or clams, an old peanutbutter jar will serve the purpose. For medium-size fish or pieces of meat, a plastic pail is good. For big pieces of meat, a 5 to 10-gallon stone crock is best. These stone crocks can sometimes be bought at a second-hand

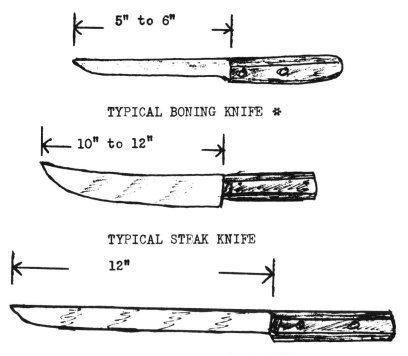

TYPICAL BONING KNIFE *

TYPICAL STEAK KNIFE

TYPICAL SLICING KNIFE

* A filleting knife is similar but frequently ½″ to ⅞″ wide and 7″ to 8″ long.

store. New ones are sold at stores specializing in restaurant kitchen equipment.

Wooden barrels or metal vessels should definitely not be used for this purpose.

### Oil

Cooking oil should be smeared on the trays or racks of a smoke oven before use. If this is not done, the meat or fish will stick to the metal.

The oil is best stored in a small bowl, and applied to the racks with a piece of cloth.

### Non-stick Spray

Commercially-made non-stick products are available in pressure cans. They are primarily meant for use in ordinary cookery, to prevent food from sticking to muffin tins, cookie sheets, frypans, etc. These products can be used to spray smoke oven racks, wire screens, perforated sheets of metal foil—anything that is used to support food for smoking. This method is more expensive than the use of oil, but it makes less work and mess. One application of the spray lasts a long time, because it does not burn off at smoke-oven temperatures. It is also much less work to clean racks and screens that have been sprayed than those that have been oiled.

## Brushes

For basting, either with oil or melted butter, a brush is useful.

A stiff bristlebrush or, even better, a wire brush, is the best tool for cleaning oven racks.

## Scales

To weigh small quantities such as brining ingredients or the seasonings for sausages, use a postal scale that reads accurately in ounces. For larger quantities such as the meats for big sausages, an ordinary kitchen scale is best. For good results every time, careful measurement of ingredients is desirable, especially at first. After gaining considerable experience, one may venture to proceed by educated guesswork.

## Thermometers

An oven thermometer to stand on the rack and show at a glance the temperature of the smoke oven is a great asset. Indeed, it is absolutely essential for a thoroughly controlled smoking process that will turn out high-quality products *every time,* and produce the finished food *on schedule.* This cannot be guaranteed without fairly exact temperature control. Oven thermometers are sold at most hardware stores.

A meat thermometer is very useful. Stick the sharp end of it into a piece of meat, and it shows when the *inside* of the meat is done—something that is hard to detect by looking at the outside of a big roast. In addition to a scale of degrees, the meat thermometer indicates "Rare", "Medium Rare" and so on.

## Extra Racks

To save time and fuel, make a spare set of racks for the smoke oven. While one batch of food is smoking, prepare the next and lay it on the spare racks, ready for a quick change-over that avoids having the oven cool down too much.

Items like oysters, clams and chicken livers are too small for ordinary oven racks; they will fall through between the bars. For such things, make a special tray of fine wire screen to sit on top of the regular rack. This tray, too, must be oiled or sprayed before use! Instead of wire screen, a sheet of heavy aluminum foil will do. Take a fork and pierce many holes in the foil to let the smoke through. This, too, must be oiled or sprayed before the food is laid on it.

### Gloves

For handling racks when the oven is on high temperature, use a pair of work gloves.

### Sausage Equipment

To make sausages—and this is a most worthwhile project—a grinder and stuffer are needed. Stuffing attachments can be bought for many of the smaller electric grinders. The chapter on sausage-making includes details on the sizes and kinds of cutters best suited for the various products.

Two or three large pans will be needed—old bread pans, refrigerator crispers or meat keepers will do—to grind the meat into, and to use for mixing the ground meat with the seasonings.

### Refrigerator

In most households the regular kitchen refrigerator is always full. It is a great convenience to have a separate refrigerator just for smoking—to store meat or fish before it is smoked, to contain the vessels during the brining of products such as corned meat or sausages that take several days, and so on.

A little care in maintaining perfect freshness of meat and fish makes the difference between a product that is just good, and one that is *excellent*.

### FUEL

Probably more arguments have raged over the question of fuels than over any other aspect of the art of food-smoking. Each region has its favorite wood. In some areas they swear by hickory; elsewhere they rave about apple, walnut and maple. Hawaiians say nothing beats guava! Let us try to establish the facts of the matter.

## Hardwoods

First, and this is one point on which all the experts agree, no wood from any kind of coniferous tree should *ever* be used for smoking food. Conifers are the firs, pines, spruces, cedars and similar trees that bear needles instead of leaves—the evergreens, to use a common expression. Conifers all contain more or less pitch. Conifer smoke will convey this pitch to the meat or fish and give it a most unpleasant flavor.

The smoke must come from hardwood, that is, wood from a deciduous tree, one that sheds its leaves in winter.

## Which Hardwood?

Some people have exquisitely sensitive taste buds. One hears, for example, of whisky-tasters who can take a sip of bourbon and tell which county the corn was grown in.

To a palate like that, there might be a noticeable difference between a hickory-smoked and apple-smoked piece of meat, especially if it had been prepared with no seasoning, or with only a salt brine.

But this book recommends various well-chosen brines and seasonings. People with palates believed to be of average sensitivity have never been reputed as able to tell the difference between one kind of wood smoke and another when the smoked food is ready for the table.

So there is really no need to fuss about what wood to use. Get any kind of hardwood that is available. Corncobs, by the way, are as good as most hardwoods. Try different kinds of wood, by all means, and if this or that wood seems to appeal to your particular taste, stick with it.

## Preparing the Wood

If the fire is made entirely of hardwood, chop or saw it into lengths short enough to go in the firebox.

To burn hardwood directly on top of a charcoal fire, cut up the branches quite small.

When using a pan on top of a charcoal fire or a hotplate, the best method is to take a hardwood branch and saw thin slices off it—as thin as can conveniently be cut with the saw. Lay a sheet of plastic on the ground, collect the sawdust, too, and use it, mixed with the slices, in the pan.

Note that at no time should the hardwood burst into flames! If it flares up, it is too dry. Soak it in water for 20 to 30 minutes before use, so that it just smolders and smokes.

It is good to accumulate a reserve supply of hardwood. But do not bring it indoors where it will become tinder-dry. Keep it outside, where it will be rained on from time to time, and will remain properly damp.

Fresh-cut, green hardwood is good. It will smolder nicely. Small twigs, even green leaves, from the tree can be used as well. They will all produce the right kind of smoke.

## Charcoal

Charcoal is now commonly sold in the form of briquets. These are made by pressing powdered charcoal, mixed with some kind of binder, into small pillow-shaped lumps. They tend to burn longer and more evenly than the raw, unprepared charcoal.

## Starting A Fire

Here is the quick, easy way to start a charcoal fire:

Take a 3-pound coffee can or some can of similar size and with a beer-can opener make some holes around the side of the can close to the bottom.

Get another container with a close-fitting top. A one-pound coffee can with plastic lid is good. So is a large-mouth peanutbutter jar. In this container put three or four charcoal briquets and cover them with a flammable liquid such as fire starter, naphtha, paint thinner, etc. Close the lid and put the jar down for a while, until the charcoal has absorbed the liquid.

In the bottom of the first can, the one with the holes punched in it, insert some crumpled-up paper. Then put the liquid-soaked briquets on this paper, light it, and fill the can with briquets.

When the whole mass is burning well, tip it into the smoke oven or barbecue. But use a pair of pliers in doing this; that can will be hot!

This method saves time. Still, most directions for barbecues say, "Start the fire 30 to 45 minutes before you begin to cook." But the described technique will produce a bed of glowing coals, ready for cooking or smoking, only five minutes after the match is struck!

CHAPTER 3

# The Key to Good Flavor:
# Brines and Seasonings

THERE ARE TWO MAIN FACTORS in successful production of smoked foods. One is correct use of the smoke oven. Heat and smoke by themselves will flavor and preserve foodstuffs to some extent. But heat and smoke are not enough.

The second factor helps to create the widest possible range of flavors, improves the texture and appearance of the finished product and, in many recipes, powerfully aids in preserving the food against spoilage. All this is achieved by the use, before, during and after the smoking process, of properly selected brines, seasonings and curative agents.

This chapter describes and gives hints for the purchasing,

storage and use of various ingredients for making good brines and seasonings.

## SALT

Common salt (sodium chloride) is a major ingredient of most brines and seasonings that are used in connection with smoke cookery and curing. Some understanding of its function will be helpful.

### Flavoring

Different people have such widely different tolerances for salt in their food that no recipe can guarantee to please every palate. The quantities of salt listed in this book will suit most people; it is recommended that the recipes be followed closely at first. However, there can be no objection, after some experience is gained, to modifying the quantities of salt (or of other seasoning ingredients) that are used in brining, curing or seasoning.

In preparing food for smoking, it is generally desirable to have the salt and other flavorings penetrate the meat or fish—the more deeply the better.

All fresh foods contain water, which holds the nutrient materials—carbohydrates, proteins, fats, minerals, vitamins—in solution, in emulsion or in the colloidal state. This water content is higher than is generally recognized. Here are some typical figures:

| | |
|---|---|
| Hard cheese | about 40% water |
| Beef | about 60% water |
| Veal, chicken, turkey | about 66% water |
| Soft cheese | about 70% water |
| Fatty fish | about 70% water |
| Non-fatty fish | about 80% water |

If dry salt be placed on the food surface, it immediately begins to dissolve in the water content, and will quickly be absorbed. This solution and absorption process takes place even if the food is apparently dry.

If brine, instead of dry salt, be applied, the process takes place in the same way. Salt from the brine mixes with the water content of the meat or fish, and penetrates towards the interior.

## Dehydration

Salt, applied to meat or fish, tends to extract water. For example, in the Brine Salting method of preservation, fish are packed in a crock with dry salt, about 1 part by weight of salt to 3 parts fish. After 2 or 3 days, the fish are found to be immersed in brine, formed by water extracted from the fish.

If fish are placed directly into an excessively strong brine, a similar action takes place; water is drawn out of the fish to dilute the brine, and the fish lose some weight.

In the Heavy Salt Cure, fish are stacked, liberally covered with dry salt. The resulting brine is allowed to drain away. The stacks are periodically turned, and fresh salt is applied. This technique will reduce the water content of fish to a little over 50%, and give it a salt content of 30%.

Nowadays—at least in small-scale operations at home—we seldom seek long-term preservation by salting or brining. For most recipes and processes, this dehydration is unnecessary. So it is best that brines be used at the recommended strengths, and that dry-salting be not prolonged much beyond the recommended times.

Keep in mind also that an excessively *weak* brine will allow the fish to absorb water at the same time as it absorbs salt. This excess water must then be evaporated by the heat of the smoke oven, so cooking time is needlessly prolonged, and the texture of the finished smoked fish may be adversely affected.

## Preservation

A salt content of 5% or more checks the growth of most spoilage organisms in meat or fish. Even smaller proportions of salt provide a noticeable preservative effect.

## Improved Appearance

When meat or fish is removed from a brine bath, certain protein constituents are dissolved in the salt water. On drying, these dissolved proteins form a thin, glossy layer at the surface. This layer, somewhat like a coat of clear varnish, is called the pellicle. It takes on an attractive coloration in the smoke oven, and is believed to aid in preservation of the smoked food.

It is usually desirable, then, that the meat or fish, on removal from the brine, be allowed to dry *before* smoking. If it is hurried straight from the brine to a hot oven, the pellicle will not form properly and the keeping qualities and appearance of the finished product will be impaired.

## Purchasing Salt

For anything more than occasional use with small quantities of meat or fish, table salt is needlessly expensive. This finely-ground, smooth-running iodized salt has no particular advantages for the purpose.

Perfectly good types of salt, at lower prices, are sold under such names as Rock Salt, Dairy Salt, Coarse Salt, Household Salt, Water Softener Salt or, in cold climates, Sidewalk Salt. Note that a similar product under the name of Ice Cream Salt is, by comparison, fairly expensive.

## Storing Salt

The mentioned cheaper kinds of salt tend, in time, to absorb moisture from the air and to become lumpy. Table salt is specially treated to prevent this. Such a lumpy consistency in no way impairs the efficacy of the salt for the purposes described in this book.

Nevertheless, for convenience in weighing, measuring and mixing with other ingredients, salt should be stored in closed packages, jars or cans, and should be protected as far as possible from excessive humidity.

## The Strength of Brine

At 68°F. 100 parts by weight of water will dissolve 35.8 parts of salt. This, the strongest brine that can be made at the temperature, is called a "saturated solution."

The strength of brine can be measured by floating in it a salinometer (sometimes called a brineometer), which looks like a glass thermometer with an oversized bulb. The salinometer floats with part of its graduated stem above the surface. The point at which the surface cuts the scale shows the strength of the brine as a percentage of saturation level.

Some people, to save trouble, simply use a saturated brine for all purposes, and keep it saturated by leaving an excess of salt lying at the bottom of the container. Such methods may result in the appearance of white salt crystals at the surface of meat or fish after it has been removed and dried. There may also be absorption of excess salt, which then has to be removed by soaking the meat or fish in fresh water—a waste of time and labor.

It is recommended that for fish the brine should generally be between 70° and 90° as measured by salinometer; 80° is a fair average.

If no salinometer is available, the following method will yield about an 80° brine. Keep adding salt—stirring to make sure it dissolves—until the solution will just float an egg or a peeled potato. Note: the potato must be fresh and juicy; if it is shrivelled or dried out, it will not be dense enough, and the brine will consequently be too weak.

The following table shows the weight of salt which, added to 1 gallon of water, will produce brines of various strengths. (Weights correct to the nearest ounce.)

| Strength of Brine | Salt per U.S. Gallon | Salt per Imperial Gallon |
|---|---|---|
| 100° | 2 lbs. 14 ozs. | 3 lbs. 7 ozs. |
| 90° | 2 lbs. 8 ozs. | 3 lbs. 0 oz. |
| 80° | 2 lbs. 4 ozs. | 2 lbs. 9 ozs. |
| 70° | 1 lb. 13 ozs. | 2 lbs. 3 ozs. |
| 60° | 1 lb. 8 ozs. | 1 lb. 13 ozs. |

A batch of brine that has served for one batch of fish or meat may sometimes be saved and used again. But, in use, it has lost part of its salt content! So it should be re-tested with salinometer, egg or potato, and should have sufficient fresh salt added to bring it up to strength again, plus a proportionate amount of the other ingredients.

However, used brine contains particles of the fish or meat which has just been removed. It will quickly go bad unless it is kept below 40°F. Even under refrigeration, its rate of spoilage will be about the same as that of fish or meat at the same temperature. So used brine should not be kept too long. Moreover, if a batch shows signs of mold, scum or bad odor, it should be discarded.

### Measuring Salt

Salt may be measured by weight, if scales are available, or by the cup. The standard measuring cup (8 fluid ounces) will hold about 10 ounces by weight of salt.

## WATER

Water varies in purity and taste from place to place. Where the local water is recognized as pure, and is pleasant to drink, it may be used as it comes from the tap. If it is heavily chlorinated, it may be boiled to expel the chlorine. Boiling will also sterilize any water that is suspected of bacterial contamination. It is not desirable to use bleach, or other chemical sterilants on water that is to be used for brining.

In regions where tap water is contaminated with detergents, or for any other reason has an unpleasant taste, it will be worthwhile to use bottled water for brine-making, especially with delicate-flavored foods such as white fish, oysters, clams, etc. As mentioned before, brine can sometimes be saved, brought up to strength, and used again. This reduces consumption of water.

## OTHER INGREDIENTS

A plain salt solution does make a useful curative and flavoring agent. It is adequate when—as in a fishing camp—nothing better is available. Yet salt alone tends to toughen meat, and certainly does not develop the best possible flavor in any meat or fish. So other ingredients, including sugar, herbs and spices, are added to enhance the flavor and tenderness of the finished product. One useful tenderizing agent is monosodium glutamate.

There should be no difficulty in getting these ingredients; names and quantities are clearly given in all recipes. Some of the flavorings, garlic and pepper, for example, are quite strong, and should be used with caution. Others are mild, and can scarcely be identified separately when the finished food comes to the table.

With all these ingredients, as with salt, there can be no dogmatic assertion that *this* quantity is right, and *another* quantity is wrong. Here, too, the road to full personal satisfaction lies through gaining experience with the printed recipes, followed by cautious experimentation with different quantities or different ingredients.

## CORRECT USE OF BRINES

Before giving any brine recipes, it is desirable to offer the following suggestions for the making and use of brines.

### Containers

Brine should never be made or stored in metal or wooden containers. Always use vessels of glass, earthenware or plastic. Stone crocks are easily obtainable. Occasionally, at a junk store, one can find large rectangular glass vessels that originally contained electric storage batteries. Hardware and department stores carry a large assortment of plastic pails, tubs, garbage cans and bowls.

## Immersion

The meat or fish must be kept completely immersed in the brine. If some pieces tend to float to the surface, they can conveniently be kept down, depending on the size of the container, by laying a saucer or plate right-side up on top of them. It may be noted that were the saucer or plate placed upside-down, air could be trapped under the concavity, and a piece of meat could rise into this air pocket. But, for a big container, cut a piece of wood to size, and weight it down with a rock or a jar of water.

## Overhauling

To obtain the best curative and flavoring effect from brining, all parts of the meat or fish must be freely exposed to the solution. Particularly if the brining crock is fully loaded, its contents must be stirred up periodically, temporarily removing some pieces of meat or fish, if necessary, to ensure that there is a thorough turnover. This rearranging of the contents of the brining crock is called "overhauling."

Overhauling also counteracts the tendency of the brine to become weaker at the top of the container as the heavier ingredients settle towards the bottom. A wooden spoon, paddle or stick should be used to reach right to the bottom of the crock and vigorously remix the ingredients.

Overhauling is unnecessary, of course, for a brief brining lasting only an hour or two, but in a prolonged cure of meat, for example, that may last two weeks or more, the meat should be overhauled every third day.

## Temperature

For short periods, up to 4 hours, the brine itself may be at room temperature, if the meat or fish is well chilled before being put in to soak. The bactericidal action of the salt will prevent tainting or spoilage.

However, in exceptionally hot weather, or in areas where tap water is rather warm, it would be a good precaution to chill the brine somewhat, and keep it chilled by hanging a plastic bag full of ice cubes in the crock. This method avoids diluting the brine as the ice melts.

When curing for longer periods, the brine should be chilled to 35°F. before starting, and kept steadily at the temperature throughout the cure, by standing the crock in a refrigerator.

## Time

Some old books and magazine articles have recommended prolonged periods of brining, followed by thorough washing and soaking in fresh water to remove excess salt. This technique is a holdover from bygone days of hard salt-curing when, without such washing and soaking, the heavily-salted fish or meat would be inedible. Nowadays, there is not the slightest advantage in putting too much salt into the meat or fish and then washing it out again. There is no advantage in allowing excessive salting or heavy brining to remove too much water from the meat or fish, and then having to replace it by soaking in fresh water.

Indeed, some expert opinion holds that excessive washing or soaking in fresh water tends to remove some of the food flavor with the salt, especially from such delicate items as white fish. The brining times recommended here will allow ample absorption of salt and other flavoring ingredients.

## After Brining

When a piece of meat or fish is removed from the brine crock, give it a quick, light rinse in fresh water, so that there will be no formation of salt crystals on the surface.

Before smoking, let the meat or fish dry at air temperature, either hanging up or lying on wire racks. Drying may be done outdoors in a light breeze (screened from flies) or indoors in front of an electric fan. Moving air gives the best results. This drying forms the glossy pellicle.

## BASIC FISH BRINE

This brine is far superior to a straight salt solution and is recommended for use with fish, oysters, clams, shrimps and prawns.

4 U.S. gallons (3⅓ Imperial gallons) water

5 lbs. (8 cups) salt

1 lb. dark brown sugar
1½ cups lemon juice
2 tablespoons liquid garlic
2 tablespoons liquid onion

Dissolve the salt first, then add the other ingredients and mix thoroughly. Test the brine with a potato or egg; the salinometer should read 80°. To be precise, of course, the salinometer is not now measuring the salt content of the brine, but shows the combined density change produced by all the flavoring ingredients.

Concerning the Basic Fish Brine, here are some suggestions:

If liquid garlic and liquid onion are not available, garlic and onion powder may be substituted, although they do not readily dissolve in water.

Alternatively, garlic cloves and onions may be crushed, but peel them first.

To peel garlic easily, cut off the ends of the clove, put it on the cutting board and press with the side of a wide knife; the skin will pop off. The garlic or onion may then be crushed with a garlic press. Or, if no press is available, place the garlic or onion in a folded piece of aluminum foil or wax paper, and crush with a wide knife or a piece of wood.

If a stronger flavor is desired, add a little tabasco sauce to the brine.

Dill may be added to the brine, for those who like it. Two tablespoons of dill salt will be about right. Alternatively, crushed or broken dill plants may be put in the brine, as they are put into dill pickles. The dill-flavored brine is particularly good for making smoked or kippered salmon.

For a subtle variation of flavor, honey or blackstrap molasses may be substituted for the brown sugar.

## BRINE FOR OCTOPUS OR SQUID (INK FISH)

4 U.S. gallons (3⅓ Imperial gallons) water
5 lbs. salt
1 lb. dark brown sugar
32 fluid ounces soy sauce
4 tablespoons monosodium glutamate
1½ cups lemon juice
2 tablespoons liquid garlic
2 tablespoons liquid onion
3 tablespoons ground ginger

Dissolve the salt first, then mix in the other ingredients. An egg or peeled potato just floats, or the salinometer reads 80°.

## DRY CURE FOR FISH

Instead of brining, especially with big fish, excellent results can be obtained by dry curing. Here is a basic formula which, by maintaining the same proportions, can, if needed, be made up in larger quantities:

2 lbs. salt
1 lb. dark brown sugar
2 tablespoons saltpeter
1 tablespoon onion powder
2 tablespoons white pepper
1 tablespoon garlic powder

Mix well, and let it stand 24 hours for the flavors to blend before use.

## SPICED DRY CURE FOR FISH

2 lbs. salt
1 lb. dark brown sugar
2 tablespoons saltpeter
2 tablespoons garlic powder
2 tablespoons crushed cloves
2 tablespoons onion powder
2 tablespoons crushed bay leaves
If a stronger spice flavor is desired, add:
2 tablespoons crushed allspice
2 tablespoons crushed mace

## SWEET PICKLE BRINE FOR MEAT

The sweet pickle cure is used for large and small cuts of meat. For shoulders and hams the pickle is often injected around the bone with a special syringe that pumps the fluid through a hollow needle. The curing may then be completed by immersion in brine, or by application of a dry cure.

Bacon can be made either with a sweet pickle or dry cure.

Ready-made, packaged sweet pickle cures are available. These cures carry instructions for use on the package.

Here is an excellent recipe, easily made up at home, that will cure up to 100 lbs. of meat:

5 U.S. gallons (4⅙ Imperial gallons) water
5 lbs. salt
1 lb. white sugar
1 oz. saltpeter
6 cloves crushed garlic *or* 4 tbsps. liquid garlic
4 ozs. pickling spices (optional)

The salinometer reading should be about 60°.

The quantity of pickling spices may be increased if a spicier flavor is desired. And, some other notes:

Prepare the spices by boiling them slowly in half a pint of water.

Keep the meat completely submerged in this solution for a time depending on the size of the pieces—from 10 days if the pieces weigh about 2 to 4 lbs. each, up to 16 days if they weigh 7 to 8 lbs. Overhaul every third day.

Inspect daily. If the pickle is kept at 35° F. there should be little risk of deterioration. But if the brine begins to change color noticeably, and to smell sour, pour it away at once, wash the meat in clean water, wash out the crock and sterilize it with boiling water. Then make a fresh batch of brine.

Many tough cuts of meat can be made tender and palatable by curing—for example, the brisket from which most corned beef is made. Bear, elk, venison, moose, etc. that is too tough to cook by ordinary methods can be turned into a real delicacy by sweet pickle curing.

## THE BRINE PUMP

This pump is like a big hypodermic syringe. The body is 7½ inches long and 1½ inches in diameter. It is fitted with a hollow needle 5½ inches long. The needle has no hole in its end. Instead, through four rows of holes in its sides, the brine is forced under pressure into the surrounding meat tissues.

The effect of pumping is to speed the process of meat curing, to make it more uniform and more certain. Right at the start of the curing process, the pump injects brine into the center of large pieces of meat, or deep into the flesh of large birds. It is used

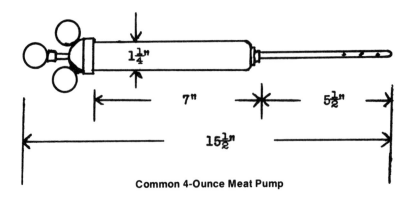

$1\frac{1}{4}$"  7"  $5\frac{1}{2}$"  $15\frac{1}{2}$"

**Common 4-Ounce Meat Pump**

especially around the bones, where a type of deterioration called "bone taint" or "bone souring" is most likely to occur. Correct use of the pump completely prevents this spoilage.

## Filling the Pump

If the pump has not been used before or has been lying empty and dry for some time, let the plunger soak in water for about 2 hours, to soften and expand the leathers. Immediately before use, sterilize the needle by holding it for 10 seconds in boiling water. Dip the needle into the curing brine, right up to the end of the main cylinder. Draw up the piston till the cylinder is full.

## Injecting the Brine

Gently but firmly drive the needle into the thickest part of the meat, near to the bone if there is any. Do not expel the entire contents at just this one location, but steadily depress the plunger and at the same time draw the needle slowly out, towards the surface. This distributes the brine all along and around the path of the needle's entry.

When the needle is finally withdrawn, some brine may begin to ooze from the hole. To prevent this, press the hole closed with the fingers until the leakage stops.

Keep the pump, especially the needle, scrupulously clean while in use. Do not lay it down anywhere, even on an apparently clean table or workbench. Do not sneeze or cough near the needle. Any such carelessness may lead to an assortment of bacteria being in-

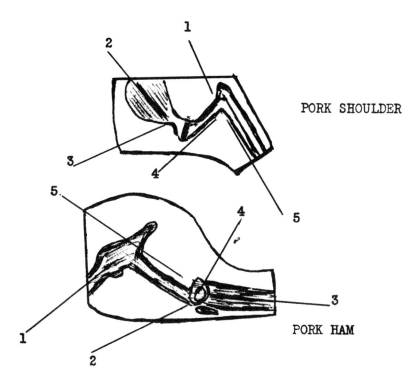

PORK SHOULDER

PORK HAM

jected into the meat, with obvious risk of spoilage. If there is the slightest risk that the needle has been contaminated, sterilize it again in boiling water.

### Quantities

About 1 fluid ounce per pound of meat will be sufficient for a mild cure. For a stronger cure, leading to a longer period of preservation, inject 1½ fluid ounces per pound. Distribute the total quantity as evenly as possible through the thickest parts of the meat.

To find the capacity of the pump being used, fill it with water and empty it into a graduated cup or jug.

### Cleaning the Pump

Do not leave the pump wet with brine. Take it apart, wash it thoroughly inside and out, and let it dry before putting it away.

## DRY CURE FOR MEAT

The dry cure can be used for many purposes instead of the brine cure. Specific suggestions are offered in later chapters.

5 lbs. salt
1 lb. white sugar
1 oz. saltpeter
2 tablespoons garlic powder
2 tablespoons onion powder

Thoroughly mix the ingredients ahead of time. Let the mixture stand, to blend flavors, at least 24 hours before use.

## BASIC SEASONING

This multipurpose seasoning can often be used to prepare meat or poultry for smoking. Suggestions for its application will be made in following chapters.

Quite apart from its functions in smoke cookery, the Basic Seasoning serves for almost any purpose in the kitchen where plain salt and pepper are being used, and gives a great improvement of flavor.

1 lb. 10 ozs. table salt
1 tablespoon onion salt
2 tablespoons celery salt
1 tablespoon garlic salt
2 tablespoons paprika
4 tablespoons black pepper
4 tablespoons white pepper
2 tablespoons dill salt
3 tablespoons monosodium glutamate
4 tablespoons white sugar

Mix thoroughly, store in a covered jar in a dry place, let it stand at least several days—the longer the better—before use. Other notes:

For a spicier flavor, 1 tablespoon of mace and/or nutmeg may be added.

For a hotter mixture, add 1 tablespoon of curry powder and/or dry mustard.

## SEASONING FOR CURED MEATS

1 tablespoon onion *powder*
1 tablespoon garlic *powder*
1 tablespoon paprika
4 tablespoons black pepper
4 tablespoons white pepper

Be sure to use the actual *powdered* onion and garlic; onion salt or garlic salt just won't do!

This seasoning is used on meat after curing and before smoking, for example in the making of jerky. The meat has already absorbed enough salt while curing—that is why this recipe contains no salt, and why garlic or onion salt should not be used.

## SMOKED SALT

This provides a delicious substitute for ordinary salt. Anytime the oven is in use for cold-smoking (not over 80°F.) put some regular table salt in a shallow pan and stand it on the oven rack. Stir occasionally to expose all the salt to the smoke. After 3 or 4 hours, depending on the smoke intensity, the salt attains a light amber color, and is then ready for use in the kitchen or at table.

# CHAPTER 4

# Smoking Butcher's Meat

ALMOST ALL MEATS MAY BE successfully cooked in the smoke oven with the full smoke treatment or, if preferred, with little or no smoke. Some cuts will turn out better if they are cured before smoking.

Correctly used, the smoke oven will produce better-tasting meals—even from the cheaper kinds of meat—than will conventional oven-roasting.

## NO-SMOKE ROASTING

The smoke oven may be used for plain roasting simply by omitting to place any hardwood chips or sawdust on the charcoal or other heat source.

Meat cooked in this way will turn out moist and succulent. The ordinary kitchen oven applies a dry heat and consequently tends to dehydrate meat or any other food that is cooked in it.

But through the smoke oven there passes a constant current of fresh air, which contains a certain amount of moisture, more or less, according to local climatic conditions. The meat is being cooked in hot, *moist* air, and therefore tends to retain more of its original water content than if it were roasted in the conventional dry-heat oven.

It should be remembered, then, that most of the following recipes can be varied, according to taste, by omitting the smoke treatment, but otherwise proceeding as recommended.

## OVEN TEMPERATURES

Long experience with the smoke oven indicates that best results are generally obtained with temperatures not over 250° F. At these moderate temperatures, cooking is rather slow and moist, and all the better for that, since it heightens succulence and flavor.

Moreover, excessively high temperatures seem to overcook the outside of a piece of meat while its inside is still raw or underdone. This might not happen in an ordinary oven when meat is in a closed roasting-pan, but it definitely can happen in an overheated smoke oven.

It is recommended, then, that no attempt be made to speed up the smoke-cooking process by overheating the oven.

## A USEFUL PRECAUTION

If the oven is hot enough to cook a meat loaf or roast, there will be a tendency for grease to drip from the meat. If this grease falls on the smoke baffle, it accumulates there until the oven door is opened and fresh air is admitted, when it flares up, with possibly dangerous results. There are two ways to avoid this risk.

Six inches below the oven rack that supports the meat, place a shallow pan, or a tray improvised by bending up the edges of a sheet of aluminum foil. The grease from this pan can be salvaged for use in other cooking operations. Its light smoke flavor will give an interesting touch to other dishes that have not been cooked in the smoke oven at all!

Make two additional baffles of sheet metal or aluminum foil, pierced with plenty of holes. Mount one of them two or three inches above the main baffle, so that it catches the drippings. When grease begins to build up on this baffle, remove it and put the spare one in its place.

## HOW MUCH IS ENOUGH?

There can be no cast-iron rules about how long meat should be smoked, because tastes differ so widely. Wherever it can be used, the best guide is a meat thermometer. Stick it into the thickest part of the meat, avoiding contact with the bone, and continue smoking until the thermometer indicates the desired degree of doneness.

Bear in mind that many smoke-roasted meats tend to be rather more red than meat cooked in an ordinary oven to an equivalent degree of doneness, especially around the bone and joints. Do not be misled by this redness, but be guided by the reading of the meat thermometer. Pork, by the way, does not show this redness around the bone and joints.

Some cuts, such as spareribs and chops, are not big enough to hold the meat thermometer. A test for these is to cut through a fleshy section and see how much red meat shows at the center, making due allowance for the expected additional redness of smoke-cooked meat.

Of course, if meat has been cured, it will stay red, like a ham, when cooked, whether it is pork or any other kind of meat.

Pork, as a precaution against trichinosis, should always be cooked until the thermometer shows Well Done, unless it has previously been frozen for 21 days at 0° F.

The flavor of the finished meat is easily controlled. For maximum smoke flavor, give a period of cold-smoking at 75° to 85° F., then heat the oven to cooking temperature until the meat is done to taste. The longer the preliminary cold-smoking, the stronger will be the smoke flavor. Times given in the following recipes will suit the average palate, but they may be extended if desired.

For a mild smoke flavor, preheat the oven to 200° to 225° F. so that the meat begins to cook at once, and remains in the smoke for a shorter time.

## BASTING

Meat that contains too little fat will require special treatment while it is being cooked. If a piece of meat obviously is short of fat, baste it with butter or cooking oil. Alternatively, one or two strips of fatty bacon may be laid on top of the meat.

If such low-fat meat is being used for making rolled roasts, insert a strip of bacon, or some beef suet, into the roast as it is being rolled.

## STORAGE OF SMOKED MEATS

All cured and smoked meats—except for thoroughly dried jerky—should be stored at 35° F. or frozen. The larger the piece of meat, as a general rule, the longer it will keep in good condition. The smaller the pieces into which the meat has been cut or minced, the more rapidly it will deteriorate.

On the other hand, the larger the piece of meat, the longer it takes to cure and to smoke. With a very large cut, the full smoke flavor may not even penetrate to the center.

These two factors should be balanced, according to what is required in each instance. If time for curing and smoking is short, cut up the meat smaller. If there is plenty of time for processing, and long storage-life is desired, leave it in large pieces.

This principle should be applied, where necessary, to modify the times for curing and smoking recommended in the following pages.

## PLAIN SMOKED MEATS

Many of the better, more tender cuts of meat may be smoke-roasted with no further preparation than a liberal use of Basic Seasoning. Sprinkle plenty of the seasoning on all sides of the meat. With rolled roast, the seasoning can be applied before the meat is rolled.

### Beef, Lamb, Pork Roasts

Apply Basic Seasoning liberally. Preheat the smoke oven to 200° to 225°F., insert a meat thermometer into the roast, and cook until done to taste.

### Steaks

Preheat the oven to 200° to 225° F. Liberally apply Basic Seasoning, and cook the steaks until done to taste, turning them over about half-way through.

Steaks will not take long to cook, so they will have just a subtle smoke flavor. But they will be moist and delicious.

### Pork Chops or Spareribs

Apply Basic Seasoning and cold-smoke at 75° to 85° F. for 1½ to 2 hours. This process should not be hurried. For a stronger flavor, cold-smoke 2 to 4 hours.

Raise the oven temperature to 250° F. and cook until the meat is thoroughly done, when chops will be gray throughout, and ribs will peel apart easily.

If the smoke oven cannot attain this temperature, the second stage may be done in an ordinary cookstove.

### Spareribs and Sauerkraut

Season and cold-smoke the spareribs as indicated in the first phase of the previous recipe. Note that this part of the process can be done well in advance, making, if desired, enough for several meals. Under ordinary refrigeration, these cold-smoked ribs will keep for 3 to 4 weeks; frozen, they will keep 2 to 3 months.

Take the sauerkraut—fresh, or a good grade of canned sauerkraut—spread it out evenly in a large, shallow baking pan, and arrange the smoked ribs on top, spreading them so that they are not piled on top of each other. Do not cover the pan.

Heat the smoke oven to 250° F. and cook until the ribs attain the desired crispness. Turn the ribs two or three times during the cooking. The drippings from the ribs will give the kraut an exceptionally fine flavor. Instead of using the smoke oven, an ordinary oven can be used, its temperature regulated to 350° F.

But watch the sauerkraut during cooking, and if it begins to dry out, pour some water on it, avoiding wetting the ribs.

One pound per person will not be too much of this recipe!

### Hearts

Beef, or any other heart, may be used. Trim the heart, removing surplus fat, cords, veins, or any other parts not wanted.

Apply Basic Seasoning liberally, inside and out. Next, stuff with a favorite dressing, as in regular cooking.

Put in smoke oven at 200° to 225° F. until well-cooked. The time will depend on the size of the heart.

### Hamburgers

Mix ground meat with Basic Seasoning, and form into patties of the desired size. Place these on a wire mesh rack, above a drip-pan, in oven preheated to 200° to 225°F. Have plenty of smoke, since the hamburgers will only be exposed to it for about 30 minutes.

Watch how the patties react to the heat. If the edges turn up, as sometimes happens, leave them alone until they are done; the slightly dished shape tends to hold melting fat, and keep the meat more succulent. With some grades of ground meat, the patties remain flat. Then there can be no objection to turning them over about half-way through.

For cheeseburgers, place the cheese slices on top of the meat patties about half-way through the cooking process.

Much can be done to vary and enhance the flavor of the finished hamburger by suitable treatment of the buns. To warm the buns, first slice them in half and butter both halves, so they will be moist. Put them in a kraft paper bag with a little water, and put in the smoke oven when the meat is about half-cooked. If there is no room in the smoke oven, put them in the kitchen oven at 225°F.

For cheeseburgers, a well-warmed bun helps to melt the cheese. And, for a richer flavor, expose the sliced, buttered buns directly to the smoke.

Chopped or minced onion, warmed in the smoke oven, may be added to the hamburger before serving, or sliced onion may be served with other relishes—mustard, ketchup, etc.

## Meat Balls, Meat Loaf

Make the meat balls or meat loaf from some favorite recipe, but replace all the usual seasoning with Basic Seasoning. Meat balls may be placed on wire racks, or arranged in a flat pan. Meat loaf should be placed in a shallow pan, to ensure adequate exposure to the smoke. Cold-smoke at 75° to 85°F. for ½ hour to 2 hours until the meat is well colored and flavored by the smoke.

Raise the temperature to 225°F. and cook until done. If the meat balls are on a rack, put a drip-pan underneath.

Meat balls may be served with spaghetti, or sliced for delicious sandwiches. For this purpose, the bread slices may be preheated and smoke-flavored as were the hamburger buns in the preceding recipe. A specially delicious spread for meat-loaf sandwiches may be made of sharp or Roquefort cheese, garlic and butter. The same spread is also excellent for hamburger buns.

## Ground Beef

Any dish made with ground beef—spaghetti, chili, Spanish rice, hash, etc.—may be given a fresh flavor if the beef is first smoked.

Spread the ground beef in a shallow pan and cold-smoke at 75° to 85°F. for 30 minutes to 2 hours, according to the strength of smoke flavor desired. Stir up the meat from time to time, so that it all gets a good exposure to the smoke.

Alternatively, the ground beef can be scattered on a fine metal screen or a perforated sheet of metal foil. In this way it would absorb the smoke somewhat faster.

### Cold Meats, Sausages, Etc.

This is not a cooking process. It will not in itself make meat ready to eat. It should be used only for meat that has already been cooked, or that is later to be cooked before serving.

Judiciously used, it will make a tasty treat out of leftover cold meats. It will greatly enhance the flavor of store-bought wieners, bologna, or other commercially-made sausages.

If uncured meat has not already been seasoned, apply Basic Seasoning. Most cured meats and all sausages will need no further seasoning at this stage.

Place on the rack, or hang up, in the smoke oven at 75° to 85°F. and leave the meat until it has attained the desired color and flavor.

### CURED SMOKED MEATS

The tougher cuts of meat will turn out much better if they are cured before being smoked. The curing softens tough meat fiber, makes the meat tender and, of course, adds much to the flavor of the finished product.

The more desirable, more tender cuts can also be cured, not to make them tender, but for a different flavor or—as in the case of jerky—to make the meat keep longer.

With cured meats, Basic Seasoning should *not* be used. The meat will have absorbed enough salt from the curing brine, and any more would be excessive. Use instead the Cured Meat Seasoning, which contains no salt.

*Important*. Meat must be chilled to 35°F. before it is placed into any brine, pickle or marinade for curing! To place warm meat into cure is to run the risk of inferior flavor, or of complete spoilage, especially if the meat contains any bone or bones.

### Beef Ribs

Place chilled short ribs in Sweet Pickle Brine and cure at 35°F. for 1 to 2 days, depending on their size and apparent toughness. Exact timing is not critical here. It is better to cure too long than not long enough. The meat will come to no harm so long as it is completely submerged and kept cool.

Remove from the pickle crock, wash lightly with fresh water, and let stand in the refrigerator until the surface is completely dry. This usually takes about a day.

Apply Cured Meat Seasoning liberally on all sides. Then cold-smoke at 75° to 85°F. for an hour or two.

Raise oven temperature to 200° to 225°F. and hold there until the meat is cooked.

## Corned Beef

Cure beef brisket in Sweet Pickle Brine at 35°F. for 2 days per pound. After curing, process just the same as beef roast. A meat thermometer will show when cooking is complete.

## Rolled Roast

Cure for 2 days per pound in Sweet Pickle Brine. Large pieces should be pumped before putting them to soak. Then remove them, wash in fresh water and leave to dry in the refrigerator.

Liberally apply Cured Meat Seasoning, and cold-smoke at 75° to 85°F. for an hour or two. Next, raise the oven temperature to 200° to 225°F. and hold there until the meat is cooked to taste.

Here are some hints for serving this cured, smoked rolled roast.

Slice very thin and serve as hors d'oeuvres. Slice somewhat thicker and make sandwiches. Dice, mix with cream sauce, and serve on toast or hot biscuits. A little sharp cheese may be added to the sauce for extra flavor.

The production of exquisitely-flavored meals from what is known to be one of the less-favored cuts of meat is one of the most satisfying and reputation-building feats of smoke cookery.

## Cured Tongue

Cure the tongue in Sweet Pickle Brine at 35°F. for 2 days per pound. Overhaul every 48 hours.

Rinse in fresh water and dry in the refrigerator. Apply Cured Meat Seasoning. Cold-smoke at 75° to 85°F. for 1 to 2 hours, according to the strength of flavor desired, then insert a meat thermometer, heat the oven to 200° to 225°F. and hot-smoke until done.

## Cured Hearts

Take any type of heart, trim and cut into strips 1" wide; cut again into pieces 1" square by whatever is the natural thickness of the meat. Hearts slice more easily if frozen.

Cure in Sweet Pickle Brine at 35°F. for about 4 hours. Then rinse in fresh water and dry in the refrigerator. Next, apply Cured Meat Seasoning.

Cold-smoke at 75° to 85°F. for 1 hour; then heat the oven to 200° to 225°F. and cook until done.

## Peruvian Cured Hearts

This method is based upon a recipe kindly supplied by Candi Palao.

Trim and cut the heart as in previous recipe. Then cure at 35°F. in this marinade:

½ cup water
½ cup vinegar
¼ cup lemon juice
1 tablespoon salt
1 tablespoon monosodium glutamate
1 teaspoon black pepper
1 teaspoon ground cummin
2 cloves garlic, crushed *or* ½ tsp. liquid garlic
1 small onion, crushed *or* ½ tsp. liquid onion

Make enough of the marinade to immerse the meat completely. These quantities will suffice for one small heart; a 3-lb. heart would require almost double the amount.

The time for marinating would depend on the thickness of the meat. A small lamb or pork heart, in which the meat is fairly thin, would be done in 1½ hours. The thick meat of a 4-lb. beef heart would need up to 4 hours.

After marinating, proceed exactly as in the previous recipe. The pieces, when cooked, may be served on picks as hors d'oeuvres. So unusual is the flavor that most people will have to ask what it is that they are eating!

## Kidneys

Beef, lamb or pork kidneys may be used. Kidneys have an outer skin or casing which is not quickly penetrated by the curing brine, so it is generally best to cut each kidney in half.

Cure in Sweet Pickle Brine at 35°F. for 2 days if halved. If uncut, leave in the brine from 3 to 8 days, according to size. Then rinse in fresh water, and allow to dry in refrigerator.

Apply Cured Meat Seasoning all over.

For mild flavor, put in smoke oven preheated to 200° to 225°F. and cook for about 45 minutes, or till done. For a stronger smoke flavor, cold-smoke at 75° to 85°F. for an hour or two, then increase the heat to 200° to 225°F. and cook till done.

Some kidneys contain very little fat. Watch them for signs of drying out, and baste if necessary with vegetable oil. Butter should not be used here; the kidneys already contain plenty of salt from the curing.

## Jerky

Nearly any red meat can be made into jerky, but for best results avoid the poorer cuts and use something like flank or round steak. Beef is commonly used, but lean lamb would serve just as well. As for pork, the jerky process does not use enough heat to provide complete protection from trichinosis, however, the trichinosis parasite can be killed by freezing at 0°F. for at least 21 days, so pork thus treated becomes safe to use.

Trim off all fat. If left on, this would eventually turn rancid. Neglect of this precaution has caused many failures for would-be jerky makers.

To save time in curing, cut the meat into slabs about 1″ thick—certainly not more than 1½″ thick. It is not the area, but the thickness of the slabs that determines the speed of the curing process. Next cure in Sweet Pickle Brine at 35°F. Allow plenty of time for curing. Four to 7 days will not be too much.

Following this, rinse with fresh water, and allow to dry under refrigeration.

Cut the meat into slices, the thinner the better, either with a very sharp knife, or a meat-slicer. To facilitate this slicing, put the meat into the freezer, and remove it when it is not quite frozen, but has a firm texture.

Apply Cured Meat Seasoning to both sides of each slice. Then hang up, or lay on racks in the smoke oven. Smoke at 75° to 85°F.—or a still lower temperature if attainable—for 24 hours, or longer if necessary. To test when the jerky is done, bend a slice. If it snaps in two, it is sufficiently dried. For a milder flavor, the jerky may be given 12 hours in cold smoke, then finished off in an ordinary oven at the lowest heat possible.

Store in a glass jar or dish with a perforated lid, or a plastic box with holes punched in the side—any convenient container which will allow air to circulate. In the refrigerator, or at room temperature, it will keep for years, if necessary, without any deterioration.

## Jerky: Quick Method

This method is farther removed from traditional techniques than the one just described, but it will produce excellent results.

Start by trimming off all fat and cut meat into slabs 1″ to 1½″ thick. Put the slabs into the freezer until they are quite firm in texture, then with a very sharp knife, or a meat-slicer, cut them into the thinnest possible slices. The thinner these slices are, the less time they will need for subsequent processing.

Put the slices in Sweet Pickle Brine at 35°F. for 30 to 45 minutes. Following this, sprinkle them with Cured Meat Seasoning. Then hang up, or lay on racks in a warm smoke oven at 85° to 95°F. until fully dried. This may take about 24 hours. For a milder flavor, smoke 12 hours and finish the drying in a warm kitchen oven.

Store in the same way as the long-process jerky.

## Smoked Cured Beef

This hard-curing process, applied to a high-quality cut of meat, will produce an exceptionally fine flavor. It somewhat resembles the jerky process, except that the whole piece is smoke-roasted, instead of being sliced, and consequently cooks without drying out.

Take a good-quality lean beef roast and cure thoroughly in Sweet Pickle Brine at 35°F. For cuts of 1 to 2 lbs., cure 3 to 5 days; for 7 to 8 lbs., cure up to 2 weeks. For faster penetration of the pickle, large cuts may be divided into pieces, each about 3″ thick. Alternatively, large cuts may be pumped for speedier, more thorough, curing.

Rinse with fresh water and leave to dry in the refrigerator. Then liberally apply Cured Meat Seasoning.

This recipe may be strong or mild-smoked. For strong-smoke flavor, give a preliminary cold-smoking at 75° to 85°F. for 1 or 2 hours (longer if extra-strong flavor is desired) and finish off at 200°

to 225°F. For mild flavor, preheat the smoke oven to 200° to 225°F. and cook till done.

Meat prepared in this way will keep perfectly under ordinary refrigeration up to 4 weeks, and freezes well.

Here are some ideas for serving:

Slice for sandwiches. Small slices on cocktail crackers, with sharp cheese, make good hors d'oeuvres.

Dice and serve with scrambled eggs, on pizzas, in salads, omelets or devilled eggs.

Serve in a white sauce (with strong cheese added if desired) on toast or hot biscuits.

### Sleight's Special Beef Sandwich

> 2 tablespoons cured smoked beef, diced
> 1 large egg
> 1 slice sharp cheese
> cream or canned milk
> Basic Seasoning
> 2 slices buttered bread

Whip the egg with the cream or milk and Basic Seasoning. Then mix in the diced beef.

Put in a small fry pan not above 300°F. Eggs may burn and, even if not burned, are less tasty, if cooked at higher temperatures.

When the mixture is firm enough, turn it over. Place the slice of cheese and one slice of buttered bread on top. When completely cooked, remove from pan and place on the other slices of bread.

## DRY CURING

Dry curing can be substituted for brine curing in many of the recipes given here. In this, as in most aspects of cookery, one cannot say authoritatively that one process is better than another—it all depends upon taste. The advocates of dry curing praise it highly, and it undoubtedly does provide some subtle flavor-differences from the equivalent brine-cured meats. Moreover, dry curing is especially useful in areas where the water is heavily chlorinated, impure, or otherwise less than ideal for human consumption.

Prepare the Dry Cure Mixture described in Chapter 3. For its use, follow the principles next detailed.

## Quantities

One pound of the Dry Cure Mixture will be sufficient to give a medium-strong cure for 12 pounds of meat.

## Application

Best results are obtained by applying the Dry Cure in two stages. Let us suppose that 12 pounds of meat are to be cured with 1 pound of the mixture.

Apply about 10 or 12 ounces of the mixture, rubbing it well into the surface of the meat. Take particular care to work the mixture in around the ends of any bones.

Refrigerate the meat at 38° to 40° F. for 4 or 5 days. Temperature control is important. Absorption of the cure is slowed down at 35° F. and ceases altogether if the meat is allowed to freeze.

Rub in the rest of the Dry Cure Mixture, and refrigerate again for at least another 2 or 3 days. Lastly, lightly wash in water and leave to dry at room temperature before smoking.

## Modifications

For a milder flavor, omit the second application of Dry Cure Mixture; wash, dry and smoke after the first application has been absorbed.

In very hot, humid climates, or if the final product is to be kept longer than usual, increase the amount of Dry Cure Mixture applied, and the time allowed for its absorption.

To develop the very finest flavor, allow the meat to season at about 35° F. for 1 to 4 weeks after washing and before smoking.

## BACON AND HAM

There is no need to devote much space to bacon and ham, since these meats are so easily available commercially. Nevertheless, the modern trend is towards a very mild cure and a very light smoke treatment, and some readers may wish to make and enjoy the incomparable flavor of some real old-fashioned bacon and ham.

## Strong Cure Bacon

For a dry cure, use the Dry Cure For Meat, 1 lb. for each 12 lbs. of bacon. Apply it in two installments, rubbing well in. Leave to cure at 38° F. for 2 days per lb. of meat; e.g., 6 lbs. are left to cure 12 days.

For a brine cure, use Sweet Pickle Brine, for the same time. Overhaul every other day.

Wash in fresh water and leave to dry at 38° F. for 24 hours.

Usually bacon receives no seasoning at this stage. But, if desired, for enhanced flavor, it may be given a light sprinkling with Cured Meat Seasoning.

Cold-smoke at 75° to 85° F. for at least 24 hours—longer for a still stronger, old-fashioned flavor.

Store-bought, sliced bacon may, incidentally, be turned into a product quite close to the old-fashioned bacon by giving it 45 minutes of intense smoke at 75° to 85° F. Compare a batch of this "improved" bacon with a batch of the ordinary bacon fried in a separate pan. There is no finer test of the difference that smoking can make to a piece of meat.

Alternatively, buy store bacon in the slab. Remove the skin, then smoke it at 75° to 85° F. for 3 to 5 hours, according to the strength of flavor desired.

The skin removed from a slab of bacon can be turned into a delicious party snack. Hang the skin in the oven and smoke it along with the bacon. Then cut it in pieces and fry in pork fat until crisp for an exceptionally tasty "crackling."

## Old-style Ham

Dry-cure or brine-cure as with bacon, but for brine cure, first pump around the ham bone. And for both cures, allow 3 days per pound of meat. Ham is thicker meat than bacon, and the cure needs more time to penetrate.

Wash in fresh water and leave to dry at 38° F. for 24 hours. Then give a thorough cold-smoking at 75° to 85° F. In a regular smoke oven, 40 hours' exposure to smoke will produce a good result. It need not be continuous, but it can be spread over 4 or 5 days if desired. In a shed smoke-house, where the smoke is much less intense, a longer period would probably be required—perhaps up to 30 days of intermittent smoking.

To the question "How much smoking will produce the perfect ham?" there can be no dogmatic answer, because different people will have widely different ideas as to what constitutes perfection! Here, as with other products, a little experimentation, with careful record-keeping, is the highroad to success.

If desired, the ham may be finished off with a period of hot-smoking at 225° to 250° F. until a meat thermometer in the thickest part shows 140° F.

This method produces ham of a quality that is unobtainable commercially, except, perhaps, in a few gourmet shops, at very high prices.

CHAPTER 5

# Smoked Poultry and Game Birds

BIRDS ARE EASY TO SMOKE. They require little preparation, and there is no difficulty in judging when they are ready to eat. They are delicious eaten hot from the oven or, with minimal care, they can be refrigerated or frozen and kept in perfect condition until required.

## CHICKEN

For those who can raise their own chickens, the ideal size for smoke-roasting is 4 to 6 lbs. dressed weight. If chickens are purchased, whole-bodied or split fryers are best, although cut-up chicken can be used.

### Splitting

Stand the fryer on the cutting block, head-end down, tail in the air, with its breast turned away from the cutting hand.

With a heavy knife, cut right down the back, and spread the carcass open. Do not turn the bird around. Cut right down the breastbone, splitting the fryer cleanly in halves. This cut is easy with a strong, really sharp knife.

## Seasoning

Liberally sprinkle both sides of each half with Basic Seasoning. If the skin is so dry that the seasoning will not adhere, moisten it with water before applying the seasoning.

## Smoking

The smoke oven should be heated to a temperature between 200° and 225°F. before the chicken is inserted. Lay the halves skin-side down on the racks. Examine the skin from time to time. When it is light amber, baste the chicken halves with butter and turn them over. Leave the halves skin-side up, and baste twice more with butter until the skin is a rich, golden amber color.

Towards the end of the smoking process, occasionally give the leg bone a gentle twist. When the bone turns easily in its socket, the chicken is properly cooked. This is an infallible test. Even if there is still a slight redness in the joint, the bird is now in ideal condition for eating.

### Use of Ordinary Oven

Some smoke ovens may not get hot enough to cook chicken properly. Then leave the fryers in the smoke oven, basting and turning as already described, until the skin is fully colored, by which time the meat is partially cooked, and the smoke flavor is absorbed. Transfer the birds to the kitchen oven, set it at 350° F., and cook until the leg bone turns easily in the socket.

For this finishing-off process, the bird should be enclosed in a covered roaster, or carefully wrapped in metal foil with the edges well crimped. These precautions will help to conserve moisture— an advantage of smoke cooking that should not be thrown away.

As an additional precaution against drying out, a tablespoon of water may be added to the foil package or roaster. A covered roaster is the more convenient, since foil wrapping hinders use of the leg-twisting test for doneness.

## Serving and Storage

Smoked chicken may be served hot or cold. Allow at least one pound per serving.

Smoked chicken, like all other poultry and game birds, keeps well when frozen—as long as 6 or 8 months with proper methods. Place each piece in a plastic bag, or wrap in aluminum foil and freeze at 0°F. Frozen, foil-wrapped chicken will keep several days after removal from the freezer, even in warm weather. It makes an excellent food to take on picnics or hunting parties.

## Reheating

To reheat frozen smoked chicken, put about a tablespoon of water in the foil package, double the edges of the foil over and crimp them tightly with the fingers. Thus the steam is kept in, the warming process is speeded, and the chicken emerges moist and succulent. Alternatively, the chicken may be reheated in a dutch oven or covered roaster, with a tablespoon of water added to ensure ample moisture.

There are some other suggestions applicable to fixing delicious chicken. For a stronger smoke flavor, start with the smoke oven at 85° to 95°F. and leave the chicken halves until they are nicely colored on both sides, then raise the oven temperature to 200° to 225°F. and complete the cooking as described above.

The half-chicken makes a convenient portion for one person. But whole chicken can be smoked just as well. So can the pieces, legs, thighs, breasts, now sold in many markets. Procedure is the same.

Apply Basic Seasoning, baste several times while smoking. Here, too, a preheated oven produces medium smoke flavor. For stronger flavor, give a preliminary cold-smoking. As with the half-birds, guard against letting the meat get dry during cooking in an ordinary oven, during cold storage, or while reheating.

Especially fine for smoking is the capon. It is more tender than other fowl; its fat is distributed throughout the lean tissues instead of being concentrated in pockets. Good capons may weigh from 6 to 8 pounds.

With home-raised chickens, it is very important to chill them promptly after killing. They are very hot-blooded birds and, if not rapidly cooled, will soon start to deteriorate.

## SMOKED TURKEY

The flesh of the turkey tends to be dry. Many a turkey cooked by conventional methods has turned out with the texture of dry blotting-paper. The smoke oven does not dry food so much as does the ordinary oven, nevertheless, careful basting is essential with turkey to keep it thoroughly succulent, and to develop the best flavor.

Turkeys are sold in several grades. Grade A birds are perfect in every part, breast, wings, skin, etc. Grade B birds may have some minor defect such as a missing wing, a humped back or a skin tear that does not affect the rest of the bird. Grade C has a more serious defect, such as skin missing from the breast. A bird could also be graded B or C for being too lean and scrawny; this lack of fat could to some extent impair the flavor, and would certainly call for extra-careful basting.

So, if it is specially desired to display the handsome appearance of the whole, smoked bird before carving, a Grade A turkey should be chosen. But if the bird is to be cut up before the diners see it, a Grade B or C turkey, carefully treated to conceal or compensate for its minor defects, will serve the purpose quite well.

### Seasoning

Liberally apply Basic Seasoning to the skin and inside neck and body cavities. Moisten the skin if necessary to make the seasoning adhere.

### Smoking

Place the turkey on the rack, breast up, with the oven at 200° to 225°F. Baste with butter or vegetable oil; about three times is usually sufficient. A wide, shallow pan should be placed about 6 inches below the turkey to catch the oil or melted butter that drips off. Stick a meat thermometer in the heavy part of the breast, not touching bone. This will indicate when the bird is cooked.

It is worth emphasizing that with turkey, as with most other smoked birds, the inner meat, around the joints, may still be red, although it is fully cooked! In this matter, trust the meat thermometer. Be guided by the taste and tenderness of the meat; do not be deceived by the red coloration.

## Use of Ordinary Oven

If the smoke oven is not hot enough to cook the turkey completely, wait until the bird has turned a rich amber and has absorbed the smoke flavor. Then lay the bird on aluminum foil; put in 4 table-spoons of water; turn up the foil, bring the edges together, fold and crimp them as tightly as possible, and wrap the foil closely around the bird. Put in the kitchen oven at 450° F. until done. This high temperature will not burn or dry out the bird if the wrapping is carefully done. The foil forms, in effect, a miniature pressure cooker which conserves moisture and cuts down cooking time.

## Serving and Storage

Serve hot or cold. A delicious sandwich can be made of sliced smoked turkey (or chicken) with mayonnaise and butter on toast.

Smoked turkey can readily be frozen whole, or whatever is left after it has been carved for a hot meal. Or it can be smoked and cut up into meal-size portions to be foil-wrapped, frozen and thawed, one by one as required. If the wrapping is carefully done, there will be no dehydration in storage.

In general, turkey hind quarters may be smoked separately. Apply Basic Seasoning on both sides. Smoke skin-side down until browned, then turn and smoke-roast until done, or wrap in foil and transfer to the kitchen oven to finish.

As with chicken, for a stronger smoke flavor, give a preliminary cold-smoking at 85° to 95°F. until the skin is well browned, then finish off at 225°F. in the smoke oven, or wrap and finish at 450°F. in the kitchen oven.

It is not customary to use dressing when smoking a turkey, but if this is desired, do not use cold dressing. In the moderate tempera-ture of a smoke oven, there is a possibility of spoilage before the dressing becomes heated above the temperature that stops develop-ment of harmful bacteria.

Here is a safe procedure. Heat the dressing in a baking dish in the kitchen oven, and stuff the turkey with the hot dressing.

Wrap in foil as described before, and place in kitchen oven at 450°F. for 1 hour or until thermometer reads 185°.

Remove foil, and put bird in smoke oven at 100° to 125°F. for about 3 hours, till it has picked up the desired smoke color and flavor.

Raise temperature to 225°F. and hold until cooking is complete.

Wild turkey, of course, gets much more exercise than the domestic variety, so it usually has less fat under its skin. It may be processed the same as domestic turkey except that, because of this lack of fat, it will require extra-careful basting with vegetable oil or butter. Bacon strips may be used instead, but they should be removed part-way through, to allow uniform browning.

If a turkey is big—over 15 lbs—start with the oven at 200°F. and quickly heat the bird right through. Then reduce temperature to 180°F. for an hour or two to let it pick up smoke. Then finish off at 225° to 250°F.

## SMOKED DUCK AND GOOSE

Domestic ducks and geese are fat birds. They need no basting and will not dry out while cooking. Wild ducks and geese are much less fatty than the tame varieties. Moreover, some people, to save the time involved in plucking, will skin a wild duck or goose, and much of whatever fat the bird carries is removed with the skin. These wild birds, then, may need basting with vegetable oil, butter, or strips of bacon.

### Plucking

Plucking is really a better procedure than skinning. Here is a quick, easy way to do it. Pick off the large feathers only, and put the partly-plucked bird in the freezer to cool.

Put a large bucket of water on a hotplate, add some paraffin, and let the water heat up till the wax is melted. Dip the bird briefly in the bucket and withdraw it. A film of solid paraffin will form on the feathers.

Repeat the dipping until a good coating of wax has built up, then put the bird back in the freezer till the wax is firm.

Crack the paraffin from the bird. If the wax coating is heavy enough, it will take off all the feathers, leaving the bird perfectly clean.

To prepare for smoking, liberally apply Basic Seasoning inside and out.

### Hot Smoking Process

Operate the smoke oven at 200° to 225°F. At this temperature, fat will drip from the bird, so arrange an additional baffle or shallow pan to catch the drippings and avoid a flare-up. Do not baste, except with skinned birds. Continue smoking until a leg turns easily in its socket, or until a meat thermometer shows "Poultry Done."

### Cold Smoking Process

This method avoids the problem of having fat dripping in the smoke oven. Smoke at 85°F. until the skin of the bird is a rich golden color. Transfer the bird to the kitchen oven at 350°F. Do not baste, except with skinned birds. The bird should not be enclosed in foil, or in a covered roaster. It should be on an open grill with a pan beneath to catch the drippings. Roast till done.

### Serving and Storage

Serve hot or cold. Dice and serve *a la king* on toast or hot biscuits, with cheese if desired. Store as with chicken.

## GAME BIRDS

These instructions will serve for pheasant, quail, partridge, prairie chicken, grouse, crow, guinea hen, sage hen, fool hen, coot or mud hen, mourning dove, pigeon (squab)—in fact, for just about all kinds of edible wildfowl.

With game birds, as with animals and fish, one cannot overemphasize the need for keeping the meat as fresh as possible. Decay can begin very soon after a bird is killed, and can proceed rapidly. Though there may be no outward signs—discoloration, bad smell, maggots, etc.—yet the flavor can soon be impaired, and there is no hope that smoking or any other process will restore it. As soon as possible after death, birds should be plucked or skinned, cleaned, washed in cold water, and hung up in a cool place to chill right through.

### Preparation

It is better to pluck the birds than to skin them. Like ducks and geese, many of these birds have immediately under the skin a layer of fat that helps to keep the flesh succulent during cooking. If a bird has been skinned, it must be watched closely for signs of drying out, and basted more often than a bird with the skin on.

If birds are much injured by shot, make a brine from 2 cups of salt in 1 gallon water. Soak the bird 4 to 8 hours to draw out the blood. Then wash in fresh water.

## Seasoning, Serving, Etc.

If a bird has been brined as just described, it has already absorbed some salt, so apply rather less Basic Seasoning than usual. Follow the directions for smoking, serving and storage as given for chicken.

## BRINE-CURING POULTRY AND GAME BIRDS

A different range of flavors can be obtained if the birds are cured before being smoked. This technique is equally good for large and small birds, for whole birds and cut-up pieces. Curing will also tenderize an old bird suspected of being tough. It is hard to tell the age of water birds such as ducks and geese, but there is an infallible test for land birds such as chicken, pheasant, partridge, quail, grouse, etc. After cleaning the bird, feel the end of its breastbone. If it bends, the bird is young. If the end of the breastbone is firm and unyielding, the bird is old. For such a bird, curing could be the better process.

## Procedure

Place the birds or cut-up pieces in a suitable container. Pour in enough Sweet Pickle Brine to cover, and weight down the bird to prevent it from floating. Keep refrigerated at 35°F.

Chicken: cure for 24 hours.

Turkey up to 12 lbs.: pump the breast and cure for 3 days.

Turkey 12 to 20 lbs.: pump the breast and cure for 5 days.

Duck and goose: cure 3 days.

Game birds: cure 24 to 48 hours, according to size.

With curing periods of more than 24 hours, overhaul and stir up the brine once or twice.

Once curing is completed, remove the bird from the brine, wash quickly in fresh water and hang upside-down in a cool place for 3 hours to dry.

Apply the Seasoning For Cured Meats, inside and out, and proceed to smoke exactly as with fresh birds.

Serve and store just as with fresh-smoked birds.

## Special Marinated Chicken Parts

As an alternative to the regular brine cure, try this recipe for chicken wings, thighs, or legs.

Prepare a marinade from the following:

⅓ cup water

⅓ cup soy sauce

⅓ cup sherry

¼ cup dark-brown sugar

½ teaspoon powdered ginger

1 tablespoon liquid garlic

1 tablespoon liquid onion

Mix ingredients in a saucepan. Warm gently to dissolve the sugar, then let the mixture cool. Immerse chicken wings in the marinade. Keep at 35°F. for 8 hours. Overhaul once or twice.

Place the wings on smoke-oven rack, and cold-smoke at 75° to 85°F. for 1 to 2 hours, depending on the strength of smoke flavor desired. Increase oven temperature to 200° to 225°F. and cook till done. During the hot-smoking period, baste the wings two or three times with some of the marinade.

Serve hot or cold.

## SMOKED LIVERS, HEARTS, GIZZARDS

Livers, hearts and gizzards of all fowl are edible, and can be made into delicious snacks or hors d'oeuvres.

For brevity, the procedure is described for livers. It may be carried out—except for some minor points to be specified—with hearts and gizzards, too. By way of preparation, carefully trim off any fat, strings, veins, etc. that may be attached to the livers.

### Scalding

This step is required for livers only. If they were simply seasoned and put in the smoke oven, many of them would stick to the racks no matter how carefully the wire had been oiled. If the livers themselves are heavily oiled before smoking, they tend to become gummy by the time they are cooked. So put a pan of water on the stove and bring it to a rolling boil. Drop the livers into the water and leave them there until no redness is visible and the surface is firmed. Remove and drain.

## Seasoning

Put some Basic Seasoning into a plastic bag. One teaspoon will be about right for one pound of livers. Put the livers into the bag. Twist the top of the bag, trapping some air, and making the bag taut like a balloon. Shake the bag so that the livers are uniformly coated with the seasoning. If the livers are still moist from scalding, the seasoning will adhere to them. If they are allowed to get quite dry, the seasoning will not adhere properly.

## Smoking

Begin with the smoke oven at 80° to 85°F. for 45 to 60 minutes. Then increase the heat to 225° to 250°F. for 30 to 60 minutes, depending on how firm a texture is desired for the finished livers.

## Oiling

The livers will be fairly dry after smoking. Put them in a wide-mouthed jar, add a small amount of vegetable oil, and roll the jar about until the livers are well coated with the oil. Leave in the jar, under refrigeration, for at least 24 hours for development of the very finest flavor.

There is an alternative seasoning method which is to put the Basic Seasoning in the water used for scalding. This will produce equally good results, but will use more of the seasoning—about 2 tablespoons for each quart of water. The seasoned water in which livers have been scalded can be saved for soup or gravy stock. Macaroni or spaghetti cooked in this water acquire a different flavor that many people find very pleasing.

Gizzards and hearts do not stick to the racks, so for them, the initial scalding step may be omitted. Otherwise, proceed as with livers, to include the final oiling treatment.

Gizzards should be cut up fairly small—into about 8 pieces each—before seasoning and smoking.

## Cured Hearts, Gizzards

To produce an interesting flavor variant, or to ensure an extra-tender texture, gizzards and hearts may be cured before smoking.

Whole hearts, and gizzards cut into eighths, should be immersed in Sweet Pickle Brine for 45 minutes. If the gizzards are left whole, brine them for 75 minutes.

Remove them from the brine, rinse briefly in fresh water, and leave in a cool place until nearly dry. Next, shake them in a plastic bag with Cured Meat Seasoning.

Smoke and oil as for uncured hearts and gizzards.

### Marinated Livers, Hearts, Gizzards

Prepare a marinade as follows:

>     1 cup water
>     1 cup of a favorite wine
>     ¼ cup salt
>     2 tablespoons sugar
>     ¼ teaspoon pepper
>     1 teaspoon liquid garlic
>     1 teaspoon liquid onion
>     1 tablespoon monosodium glutamate

Before marinating, scald livers, and cut gizzards into eighths; hearts may be processed whole. Marinate for 8 hours at 35°F.

Spread out on a wire screen. Smoke for 30 minutes at 75° to 85°F. Raise temperature of smoke oven to 200° to 225°F. and cook until done to taste.

## SPECIAL DISHES WITH SMOKED LIVER

Smoked chicken livers can be used as the basic material for making other dishes. Here are some recipes.

### Smoked Liver Stuffed Eggs

>     12 hard-boiled eggs
>     ½ lb. smoken chicken livers
>     2 teaspoons chopped green onions
>         (including a little of the green tops)
>     ½ teaspoon salt
>     ¼ teaspoon pepper
>     1 teaspoon bacon fat

Cut the hard-boiled eggs in half, and carefully remove the yolks. Mix the egg yolks, smoked livers, green onions, salt, pepper and bacon fat. Run them through an electric blender to a smooth, paste-like consistency.

Stuff the mixture into the halved egg whites, and chill. Before serving, garnish with cross-sliced ripe or stuffed olives.

## Smoked Liver Paste

1 lb. smoked chicken (or goose) livers
2 hard-boiled eggs
2 medium onions
1 teaspoon dried herbs
Salt and pepper to taste

Shell and chop the hard-boiled eggs. Coarsely chop and sauté the onions. Chop the livers finely.

Mix eggs, onions and livers, and season with the herbs, salt and pepper.

To make the paste, put through a meat grinder, or mash with a wooden spoon or heavy fork.

Use of a blender for the final step is *not recommended;* it does mash up the ingredients, but tends to produce a texture that many people would consider too soft and sloppy.

## Smoked Paté De Foie Gras

½ cup smoked chicken livers
2 tablespoons chicken fat (or butter)
¼ medium onion
Mustard or celery salt to taste
Salt and pepper to taste

Finely chop the onion and sauté in the fat until it is yellow. Then chop the liver fine.

Mix the ingredients and season to taste. Put them next through a meat grinder, or mash with a wooden spoon or heavy fork.

Place at once on ice.

CHAPTER 6

# Smoking
# Wild Game

HUNTERS ANNUALLY WASTE ENORMOUS
quantities of wild game meat by failing to keep it fresh in the field.
Many of them do not realize how delicious the various varieties of
game meat can be when properly smoked. Meat that is too tough
for grilling or roasting can be made tender by appropriate curing.

So game meat can be conserved. It can be made into delicious,
money-saving meals and the hunter can gain additional pleasure
and personal satisfaction by proving himself not only a good shot,
but a good cook, too.

## IN THE FIELD

Curing and smoking can help preserve game meat, and can give it
a whole range of delicious flavors. But these processes will not

work miracles. They cannot salvage meat that is really not fit to eat!

Before investing time and labor in smoking game meat, consider a few questions. Has the rutting season just started? Does the buck have a swelled neck? Or is it a dry doe? Was it downed by a clean, quick shot? Or was it shot through the belly, so that it ran a long way, with resulting destruction of the intestines and contamination of much of the meat? Did the bullet hit a heavy bone, disintegrate and tear up half the meat?

Mangled, bloodshot, tainted or otherwise inferior meat is not worth bringing to the curing-crock nor the smoke oven. It will do no credit to the smoking process, or to the hunter.

Reasonable care in selecting good meat and in looking after it properly will be repaid by greater ease in the curing and smoking, greater pleasure in the eating, and greater pride in serving the meat to family and friends. There will be no more complaints about the so-called "strong" flavor of game meat, but the people who thought they did not like it will be coming back begging for second helpings!

## Promptness, Cleanliness

Get the meat cooled down as soon as possible after the kill. Heavy-skinned animals should be skinned immediately, to speed this cooling.

Keep the surface clean. If, after skinning, much hair adheres to the meat, or much blood is drying on it, wash with a solution of 1 part vinegar to 20 parts water. This will dislodge the hair and remove the blood.

Keep insects off the meat; cover it with a game bag if necessary.

With these precautions, in fairly cool temperatures, game will keep in good condition for several days, and can be brought home in top shape for further processing.

## Smoking

For smoking in the field, it is easy, with boxes, branches, plywood, canvas or sheet plastic, to make one of the temporary smoke ovens described in Chapter 2. Once the oven is built the actual smoking can be done on the spot.

## CURED SMOKED VENISON

The method described here will also serve in general for the meat of other game animals—moose, elk, bear, wild pig, raccoon, cougar, goat, etc. Special pointers for handling some individual kinds of meat are mentioned in the remarks that follow the general instructions.

Cure the meat in Sweet Pickle Brine from 5 to 12 days, depending on the size of the pieces. Pump big pieces, especially those containing large bones, before putting in the brine crock.

Remove from the brine and wash quickly in cold water. Let dry for 24 to 48 hours at 38°F. Then sprinkle liberally with Seasoning For Cured Meats.

Cold-smoke at 75° to 85°F. to give a rich smoke flavor. The time allowed for this cold-smoking cannot be stated as "so many minutes per pound." Consider two pieces of venison, each 5 lbs. in weight. One has a thick, compact, cylindrical shape, the other is a thin, flat slab. Obviously the thin, flat piece will be penetrated and flavored by the smoke much faster than will the thick piece. So, as a rough guide, allow 30 minutes' exposure to moderately dense cold smoke for each inch thickness of the meat. For example, a slab 3-inches thick gets 90 minutes' cold-smoking.

Then, with oven temperature 225° to 250°F., roast until a meat thermometer shows the required doneness. If the meat seems to be drying out, baste it occasionally with cooking oil. If the meat is very fat, put a pan six inches under the rack to catch the drippings.

If the smoke oven will not attain 225°F., finish off the cooking in a covered pan in the kitchen oven at 350°F.

### Fat Content

Butcher's meat is fairly uniform in its fat content whereas wild game may vary very widely, and consequently needs special attention.

Many people dislike venison fat, so venison generally has all the fat trimmed off before processing. Then, for the hot-smoking stage, it needs liberal basting with cooking oil. Alternatively, strips of bacon can be put on it.

Bear is another fat meat, but the fat does not seem to be so widely disliked, so some or all of it may be left on. Bear meat, like pork, is subject to trichinosis. Therefore, like pork, it must always be cooked until well done, or else frozen for 21 days at 0°F. before cooking, to kill the parasite.

Elk and moose provide dry meat. These roasts should be basted frequently, or well laced with bacon.

## Dry Curing

Instead of the brine cure first described, a dry cure can be used. Follow the method described for butcher's meat in Chapter 4. At the end of the prescribed curing period, wash with cold water, then dry for 24 to 48 hours at 38°F., sprinkle liberally with Seasoning For Cured Meats, and cold-smoke at 75° to 85°F. for a rich smoke flavor as already detailed. Follow by roasting as initially explained.

## Serving

Slice the cured, smoked meat very thin, and serve in sandwiches, on cocktail crackers, with sharp cheese, or with some favorite savory spread.

Other suggestions: dice and mix with cheese for a spread. Or, dice and cook in scrambled eggs or gravies. Another: serve in white sauce on toast or hot biscuits, with sharp cheese added.

## Modifying Recipes

Wild game varies much more widely than butcher's meat, not only in fat content as described above, but also in age, toughness, and intrinsic flavor based upon whatever diet the animal has followed.

No standard recipe can accommodate all the possible range of variations in fatness, texture and flavor. But there is no doubt that by suitable control of curing methods and times, amounts of seasoning, times and temperatures of smoking, and methods of serving, most kinds of game meat can be made exceedingly palatable. So here again, thoughtful experimentation, combined with careful record-keeping, will be the key to success.

# SMALL GAME ANIMALS

These suggestions can be applied to most small game animals such as rabbit, hare, squirrel, muskrat, porcupine, ground hog, etc.

Apply Basic Seasoning liberally, both outside and inside the body cavity. Cold-smoke at 75° to 85°F. for 1 to 2 hours, according to the strength of flavor desired. With oven temperature at 225° to 250°F., roast until done. Some of these animals have little fat, so they will need careful basting with vegetable oil, butter or bacon strips.

For a different flavor, these small animals can be marinated before smoking. Use the marinade recommended for chicken livers, hearts and gizzards in Chapter 5. For rabbit and hare, a dry red wine is generally favored. Marinate 8 hours; then smoke as described above.

## JERKY

Bear, moose, deer—in fact, most game animals, will make excellent jerky by either of the methods described in Chapter 4.

## HEARTS

Many wild animals have hearts larger for their size than those of similar domestic animals, probably because they get so much more exercise in obtaining their food and fleeing their enemies. Game hearts are often neglected, but they can be prepared just the same as, and will taste just as good as those of domestic animals. See instructions for use of hearts in Chapter 4.

## TONGUES

Game tongues can be cured, seasoned and smoked just like the beef tongue described in Chapter 4.

# CHAPTER 7

# Smoked Fish and Shellfish

SOME STORES NEVER SELL, AND some people never see, any other smoked fish besides salmon and kippered herring. So it is worth emphasizing that the smoking process can be very widely applied. Here, for example, is a list—certainly not all-inclusive—of some kinds of fish that have been successfully smoked.

Saltwater Fish

| | |
|---|---|
| Bonefish | Grouper |
| Mullet | Sandfish |
| Mackerel | Snapper |
| Bonita | Grunt |
| Tuna | Porgie |

| | |
|---|---|
| Pompano | Cod |
| Snook | Flounder |
| Sea Bass | Halibut, etc., etc. |

Freshwater Fish

| | |
|---|---|
| Bass | Catfish |
| Crappie | Carp |
| Bream | Whitefish |
| Trout | Shad |
| Pickerel | Sturgeon |
| Northern Pike | Grayling |
| Muskellunge | Walleye, etc., etc. |
| Perch | |

This chapter explains the basic curing and smoking methods for fish and shellfish, and also describes a number of special techniques for individual species.

## HANDLING FISH

Fish is so delicate in texture and flavor that it can easily be spoiled by careless handling. Here are some hints for the treatment of fish before, during and after smoke processing, that will help to develop the finest possible flavor, and to ensure perfect preservation.

### Treat Fish with Care

In every operation—transportation, cleaning, splitting, salting, hanging, storing, etc.—fish should be handled as gently as is practicable. When a fish is caught, kill it at once cleanly. If it is allowed to flop around in the bottom of a boat, it is already getting bruised. When cutting fish, use a very sharp knife, and so avoid bruising or tearing the flesh.

### Keep Fish Cool

After a fish is landed, decomposition begins almost at once, especially in the internal organs, and the resulting chemical action tends to warm the flesh. If its temperature is allowed to rise above 70°F., a fish will be spoiled in an hour or two. So keep fresh-caught fish in a cool place, preferably in the shade. Direct sunlight warms the fish and speeds decomposition. Smaller fish may be put overboard on a stringer, in a fish basket, a burlap bag, or a mesh onion net, until ready to go ashore.

Preferably the fish should be kept about 35° F. until the actual smoking is begun. When fishing through ice, of course, there is no problem in keeping fish in good condition all day.

## Cleaning Fresh-caught Fish

If possible, clean fish as soon as it is killed. The common practice of leaving fish lying uncleaned in a boat or on the ground, for several hours, greatly increases the risk of spoilage. Even if the fish, in these circumstances, does not become noticeably tainted, there is a certain loss of the fine, delicate flavor that goes with perfect freshness.

Clean the outside of the fish. Scrape off the scales with the back of a knife, or some other suitable tool. Not all fishermen would agree with this recommendation for prompt de-scaling, yet there can be no doubt that removal of this protective layer does aid in rapid cooling of the fish. A garden hose will scale larger fish.

Also scrape and wash off external slime. A mixture of 1 part vinegar to 4 parts water will be useful for this; alternatively, use a stiff bristle brush under running water. Then give the fish a quick rinse in cold water.

For small fish, and for a few special purposes described later, the head may be left on. But, as a general rule, cut off the head at once. Do not cut too far back; leave the bony plate or collarbone beneath the gills. This makes a convenient, firm support if the fish is to be hung up at any stage of processing.

With large fish, cut off the tail. For small fish, leave the tail on. It helps to keep this end of the fish from drying out too much.

For large fish, remove the fins. Cut around the base of each fin with a sharp knife and pull it out, using pliers if necessary. Removal of fins is unnecessary for small fish such as smelt, perch, crappies, sunfish, etc. They will smoke more uniformly, having no holes in the body.

Small fish, such as the perch, crappies and other species just mentioned can very well be smoked in the round. But bigger fish should be split, either along the belly or along the back, according to the procedure to be used. Remove the guts and gills. Thoroughly wash to remove every trace of blood, guts, black skin and gills. A brush is handy for this internal cleaning. For smaller fish, a toothbrush serves well. Large fish should be hung up, head-end downward, to speed the draining of blood.

Fish less than 1-lb. weight can be gutted without splitting by a method called "gibbing." Make a small cut on the bottom centerline, behind the jaw, below the gills. Insert the thumb and finger, pull out the guts and gills and wash the body cavity thoroughly with cold water.

Keep the cleaned fish as cool as possible until they can be processed.

## Storing Unprocessed Fish

If fish must be held for any long time before smoking, they should be frozen. Here are some hints.

The ice-cube compartment of an ordinary refrigerator will not give sufficiently low or sufficiently constant temperatures for good fish freezing. For this purpose, the fish must be brought quickly to a temperature of 0°F. or lower, and must be kept there without variations. A proper deep-freeze unit, preferably with a special quick-freeze compartment for the preliminary rapid cooling, will give best results.

Small fish may be put into a milk carton of water and frozen into a solid block of ice. A weak salt solution—⅓ cup of salt to 1 gallon water—is even better than fresh water for this purpose. Thus frozen, fish will keep in excellent condition for an indefinite period so long as they are never allowed to thaw.

To freeze a larger fish, place it on a cookie sheet or a sheet of waxed paper until it is frozen hard. Then dip the fish into a pail of water chilled with ice cubes. This puts a glaze of ice on the fish. Repeat the freezing and dipping several times, to produce a thick, strong glaze. Then place the fish in a plastic bag, or wrap it in waxed paper. Fish prepared this way may be stacked in the freezer and will not stick together, so one or more may be taken out and used at any time without injuring the others. This same method is handy for smaller fish, too, if they are likely to be used one, or a few, at a time.

When the fish are to be used, thaw them, and smoke them according to the instructions for fresh fish. If this freezing is carefully done, with gentle handling at all stages, no one will be able to detect any difference, after smoking, between the frozen fish and fresh-caught fish.

## Splitting and Filleting

To split a fish open, cut it down the back, just to one side of the backbone. Leave the belly skin uncut, as a "hinge" on which to open up the fish. This splitting exposes a maximum area of flesh to the brine, seasoning and smoke.

Large fish may be further divided into fillets. For this purpose, remove the head and tail, split down the back, cutting the belly skin as well, so that the fish is divided into separate halves. Remove the backbone by a second cut on the other side of it. Cut the halves into fillets of the desired size.

The skin should be left on big fish such as striped bass, salmon, sturgeon, etc. to give the fillets greater strength during processing, and to retain the flavor which some people believe lies in and immediately under the skin.

## Storage of Smoked Fish

A general rule for storage of smoked fish is that the drier it is, the longer it will keep. The best technique is to wrap each fish separately in waxed paper or aluminum foil and refrigerate at 35°F.

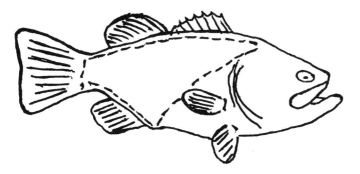

**How To Fillet A Fish**

If fish is to be smoked, scale first, then with a thin-bladed knife such as a boning knife, slit the skin on the dotted lines as shown above from the head along the top of the back to the tail fin. Cut the skin from the head to the lower fin or anus, and extend to the tail.

Next, grasp the fish by the tail and with a wider knife such as a slicing knife, held against the backbone of the fish, slice toward the head, and end up with a nice fillet. Turn fish over and do the same.

Most smoked fish should not be frozen. Admittedly, freezing prevents decay, but, on thawing, the fish may be found to have lost much of its flavor, and to have acquired an unpleasant, pulpy texture. The only smoked fish that can be successfully frozen is a hard-smoked one that contains very little moisture.

## DRYING

We are not concerned here with lengthy, old-fashioned drying processes—exposing fish to the wind for weeks, to obtain a practically incorruptible product, dry and hard as a board.

Nevertheless, it is desirable that after brining or salting, fish should be allowed to dry before smoking. First, this drying forms the pellicle. Second, if fish are smoked while wet, they may soften just as they do in the ordinary steaming process and fall apart instead of retaining their shape and a pleasantly firm texture.

After removal from the brine or salt, give the fish a *quick* rinse in fresh water, then hang up to dry in a cool, breezy, shady place protected from flies. If the fish are hanging indoors, an electric fan may be used to keep air moving over them.

Inspect the fish occasionally. When the surface is completely dry and the hard, shiny pellicle is fully formed, they are ready for smoking.

If it is inconvenient to hang the fish up, they can be dried on wire racks or oven-grids. Fillets should be skin-side down. At this stage the wire will make an impressed pattern on the fish, and it looks better if this is on the skin rather than on the flesh side.

Alternatively, the wet fish can be hung up or laid on racks in the smoke oven. Air is kept moving through the oven by a fan, or by application of a low heat—not above 80° F.—until the pellicle has formed. For a mild flavor, this drying is done without smoke. For a stronger flavor, smoke may be used at this stage.

Drying, and formation of the pellicle, usually takes about three hours.

## SMOKE OVEN OPERATION FOR FISH

Here are a few technical points that will aid in easy, efficient fish smoking.

### Fish with Heads On

Hang the fish from a stick, or from nails, by S-shaped wire hooks. If the hook is put in the mouth, be sure it goes under the jawbone

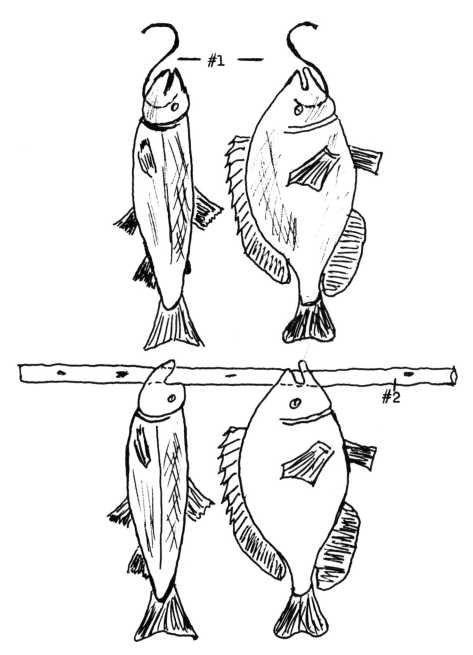

**Methods of Hanging Fish for Smoking**

#1—Wire "S" hooks
#2—Green stick or iron rod

for firm support. If it is put through a gill-slit, get it under the collarbone. Despite all precautions, the fish may soften somewhat as it is smoked. If the hook is bedded only in the flesh, it may tear loose and let the fish fall.

A thin stick, or thin iron rod, may be pushed in at the gill-slit and out through the mouth. A number of small fish can thus be threaded on one stick or rod, so long as they are spaced far enough apart that the smoke can circulate freely around them.

## Split Fish

Split fish must be supported so that the smoke can reach every part of the surface.

Fish that have been split down the belly for removal of the gut can be hung by S-hooks passed under the collarbone. But the sides of the belly, under the influence of heat, might curl inward and prevent smoke from circulating in the abdominal cavity. As a precaution, take a thin, short stick, pointed at both ends, and wedge it crosswise between the two flaps of abdominal flesh, to hold the cavity open.

Fish that have been split open and flattened out may be hung by two S-hooks at the upper outside corners, or they can be fastened with small nails to wooden crosspieces. It is not good enough to drape these fish over a horizontal stick. The two down-hanging sides may bend until they touch, and so prevent free access of the smoke. Two horizontal sticks should be placed about an inch apart, and the fish hung over *both* sticks, so that the down-hanging sides are kept well separated. Alternatively, the fish can be placed on wire racks.

## Fillets

Fillets should be laid on racks, skin-side down.

## Turning

Whole fish on racks may be turned over half-way through smoking. This turning is not essential to the cooking process, but it does help to give more uniform coloration.

Fillets should not be turned over, but left skin-side down until done.

### A Harmless Phenomenon

If a fish has been insufficiently dried after brining so that the pellicle is not properly formed, then while it is being smoked, a white liquid may ooze from the surface. This is not in any way harmful or unpleasant. It is a mixture of tasty, nutritious protein substances that normally form the pellicle. Do not try to remove this secretion. Simply let it solidify on the surface of the fish.

### Smoking Times and Temperatures

Specific instructions as to times and temperatures are given in the recipes that follow, but some general principles should also be mentioned.

Cold-smoking—not above 85°F.—is generally favored for fish that are to be preserved for a long time. A preliminary period of cold-smoking may also be given, to impart a stronger smoke flavor to fish that are later to be hot-smoked.

Hot-smoking—between 85° and 250°F.—is in effect a cooking process. Hot-smoked fish are usually intended to be eaten immediately or, at most, to be kept for 2 or 3 weeks under refrigeration.

Fish that are to be canned should be given a fairly brief smoking, just enough to give the desired flavor and color. Canning seems to intensify the smoke flavor, and anyway, cooking will be completed during the canning and sterilization processes.

### Basting

Some fish contain plenty of oil and will remain succulent during smoking. Others—bass and perch, for example—contain very little oil. Such fish should be basted with cooking oil to keep them from drying out, and to enhance their flavor.

### Extra Seasoning

A good variant flavor may be obtained by sprinkling pepper on the fish immediately before it is put into the smoker. To save space, this fact is *not repeated* in every recipe, but the pepper may be used whenever desired.

## BRINE PROCESS

Probably the most-used process for fish is to immerse them in brine for a time before smoking. This section offers some general hints for brine-smoking, also specific instructions for processing various kinds of fish and shellfish.

### Time of Brining

It was pointed out in Chapter 3 that nowadays we seldom give food a high salt content as a means of preserving it for a long time. The light or moderate brining or salting now used serves three main purposes:

It firms the flesh by removal of moisture.

It has sufficient preservative effect to prevent spoilage during drying or cold-smoking processes, where the fish may remain for some time below ordinary cooking temperatures.

It gives the required taste. This function is most noticeable to the person eating the finished product. So, especially in delicate-flavored fish, the degree of saltiness produced by brining or dry-salting must be accurately controlled.

If brine is made up at random, to a different strength on each occasion, one obviously cannot guess how long it will take for a piece of fish to absorb the desired amount of salt. With two variables—brine strength and time—the process is out of control, and there can be no guarantee of success.

But if brine is always made up exactly to the recommended strength, and if the soaking time for each batch of fish is recorded, then complete control is easily attainable. Suppose a batch of shrimp, after 20 minutes' brining, proves to be just a little too salty for the family's taste. It is simple to determine that the next batch, in the same standard brine, should be immersed only for 15 minutes.

So the method is this; always use the standard-strength brine that is recommended for each kind of fish. To control the degree of salt absorption, vary the time of immersion.

In smoke cookery, as in other arts, there can be no rigid rules, but the following table will serve as a guide when preparing fish for hot-smoking—to be cooked in the smoke oven for immediate consumption, or for a short period of storage.

These times apply to fish usually recognized as lean or non-oily, such as flounder, Gulf grouper, halibut, buffalo carp, perch, sun-fish, crappie, bream, sea bass, mullet, pickerel, pike, muskellunge, etc.

| Weight of Fish | Time for Brining |
| --- | --- |
| Under ¼ lb. | 30 minutes |
| ¼ lb. to ½ lb. | 45 minutes |
| ½ lb. to 1 lb. | 1 hour |
| 1 lb. to 2 lbs. | 2 hours |
| 2 lbs. to 3 lbs. | 3 hours |
| 3 lbs. to 4 lbs. | 4 hours |
| 4 lbs. to 5 lbs. | 5 hours |

If the skin is left on a fish, the brine ingredients cannot penetrate so fast, so increase brining time by 25%.

For oily fish such as Great Lakes chub, Atlantic herring, Gulf pompano, most trout, whitefish, cod, mackerel, salmon, sturgeon, dogfish, etc., increase brining time by 25%.

If, on a thick piece of fish, the flesh has been scored with a knife to assist penetration of the brine, reduce brining time by 25%.

If a 4-lb. fish has been split, and the two halves remain con-nected by a flap of skin or a thin piece of flesh, it obviously should be treated as two 2-lb. pieces, and brined accordingly. The original weight of a big fish is irrelevant. Calculate times by the weight of each side, fillet or chunk that is exposed to the action of the brine.

When brining a number of fish or pieces of different sizes, it will be convenient to keep them in different containers, roughly graded by sizes, then each batch may be put in and taken out together, so that no piece receives too much or too little brining. A batch of smelt in the round, for example, may be done in 30 minutes. Another brine crock, full of bigger fish, can stand for 2 hours while the smelt are being further processed.

## Time of Smoking

After removal from the brine, the fish are dried to form the pellicle and then placed in the smoke oven. For smoking, as for brining, there are no rigid rules, but the following principles will be helpful.

For hot smoking:

Inspect the fish from time to time, pressing it gently with a knife or fork. When it begins to separate into flakes, it is done.

Thick pieces of fish may appear to be done outside while the center is not yet cooked. To overcome this problem, use a meat thermometer. When the center of the fish is at 140°F. it is fully cooked.

For oysters, clams and similar seafoods that do not flake when cooked, the best test is to take one from the oven and taste it.

Prawns, shrimps and crayfish (crawfish) turn a characteristic red or orange color when cooked.

For cold smoking:

Follow the general time guides given later in this chapter. Inspect the fish occasionally to see when it has the desired color. The time this takes depends largely on the smoke density. Cold smoking is generally undertaken as a preservative technique. Its efficacy depends on *drying* the fish, so it is safer to give the fish a little too long in the oven rather than to remove it too soon. If the desired color is attained prematurely, remove the hardwood from the smoke generator, and let the drying proceed with no smoke. If the fish is thoroughly dried, and yet is not properly colored (which also means that it is not yet properly *flavored*), add more hardwood and finish the process with a period of exposure to a heavy smoke.

## BRINE CURE—HOT SMOKING

These instructions may be applied to all kinds of fish.

### Cleaning

Remove exterior slime and scales. With catfish, bullheads and other fish that have no scales, remove the slime, but leave the skin on. With most fish, cut the belly open, remove guts and thoroughly clean the body cavity. Small fish may be gibbed.

### Trimming and Cutting

For small fish that are to be smoked in the round, leave fins and tails on, and the head, too, for convenience in handling and hanging up. For a big fish, cut off the fins and tail. If it is to be cut in halves, fillets or chunks, remove the head.

If the fish is to be split, lay it on one side, start at the head and, with the knife scraping the top of the backbone, cut it in half. For small and medium-size fish, leave a strip of back or belly skin intact, holding the halves together. Then, after smoking, the halves can be folded back into their original position to look like a whole fish for serving.

For bigger fish, separate the halves. Make another lengthwise cut just under the backbone, and remove the bone. Then cut the halves lengthwise into fillets or crosswise into chunks for processing.

### Brining

Put the fish or pieces in the Basic Fish Brine, preferably at a fairly cool temperature. In very hot weather, keep the brine cool by hanging in it a plastic bag of ice cubes. Put a plate or some other flat object on top of the fish to keep it submerged. Leave it for a time proportional to its weight. In a brining of more than 2 hours, overhaul once.

### Rinsing, Drying

Take the fish from the brine and rinse *briefly* in fresh water. Hang it up or lay it on racks to dry in a cool, airy place, screened from flies, while the pellicle forms. Omitting the procedure will produce the "harmless phenomenon" previously described, and will necessitate a longer period of smoking, since the oven then has to draw more moisture out of the fish.

### Smoking

The smoke oven should be at 75° to 85°F. and the smoke generator in action by the time the fish is dried. Hang the fish or put it on the racks in the oven. If using racks, grease or oil them lightly, so that the fish does not stick. Note the time. Allow a period of cold-smoking proportional to the strength of smoke flavor desired. Then raise the oven temperature to 125° to 150°F. Check smoke density periodically. Test fish to see when it is done. Note the time required for complete cooking.

### Storage

Remove and serve; or, if the fish is to be stored, let it cool, wrap tightly in metal foil or waxed paper, and refrigerate at once.

## Salmon

Here are some special hints for the processing of salmon.

Never remove the skin from salmon. Leave it on, whether the fish is processed whole, in halves, or in smaller cuts.

For salmon, the blackstrap molasses variant of the Basic Fish Brine gives particularly tasty results.

Another delicious variant is to cut short the brining period by half an hour, and then marinate the fish in soy sauce for 30 minutes before drying and smoking.

It is easy to produce what is sold commercially as "kippered salmon." This is made in exactly the same way as ordinary smoked salmon except that after brining it is colored with a harmless dye, to give it the attractive reddish color. Some people put the dye in the brine; but then that batch of brine is spoiled for regular use. It is more economical to use a separate dye bath.

Kipper coloring is sold under various trade names, but the actual coloring ingredient is usually 150 Orange I, a dye approved under the U.S. Federal Food and Drug Cosmetic Act. Half an ounce of the dye mixed with 2½ U.S. gallons of water (2⅛ Imperial gallons) makes a suitable strength. Dip the fish for 15 to 30 seconds, according to the depth of color desired.

Ordinary food coloring may be used instead, but it does not give such a rich color.

## Eels

Gut and clean, as with fish. Brine for about 1 hour. Rinse briefly in fresh water.

Dip for a few seconds in boiling water. This will make the body cavity open up.

Smoke at 140°F. for 2 to 4 hours, according to size.

## Octopus

Octopus meat is too tough to be processed like other sea foods, but, by using the technique described here, it can be made as tender as a piece of chicken.

Cut open the body and remove the digestive organs.

Boil the octopus until a fork can easily be put into the tentacles.

Cool the octopus. On a big octopus—up to 30 or 40 lbs., like some caught in Puget Sound—the dark skin can be unpleasantly tough so it should be peeled off at this stage. If possible, leave the suction cups in place. They make an interesting feature on the finished product.

On a small octopus—3 to 4 lbs., like those imported from Japan—the dark skin is not tough, and may be left on.

Cut the tentacles crosswise into slices about ½ inch thick, Cut the body into chunks about the same size as those obtained from the tentacles.

Put all the pieces in the special Octopus Brine for 1 hour.

Remove from the brine and leave in a cool place until the slices are dry.

Place on oiled grids and smoke at 125° F. until nicely browned.

The octopus is now ready to eat. Many people enjoy it like this. However, if a richer flavor is desired, use the oiling process described next.

Put the sections of smoked octopus into a container with a lid, such as a big glass pickle jar. Add some olive oil or cooking oil, screw down the lid, lay the jar on its side and keep rotating it until the octopus pieces are all coated with a shining layer of oil.

After a few minutes, the oil will have been absorbed into the pieces. Rotate the jar again to distribute the oil afresh. Keep adding more oil as the original supply is exhausted. Continue the process until the octopus will absorb no more oil. This may take an hour or more of intermittent attention.

Now the oiled segments are ready to eat. If any are left over, they may be kept under refrigeration for several days, or may be canned.

### Oysters

Considerable labor can be saved and the finished product much improved by correct treatment of oysters before smoking. Here is the best way to proceed.

Fresh oysters in the shell:

Do *not* try to shuck the oysters by breaking the shells. Use a knife, or put them in the top of a steamer and steam until the shells open. Then pick out the oysters, firm-fleshed and undamaged. Alternatively, put the shells on the rack of the kitchen oven or of the smoke oven, with the cup-side down, to conserve moisture. Heat until they open. With this method, place a pan under the rack to catch the water that drips out of the oysters.

Store-bought oysters, out of the shell:

Put them in the top of a steamer, or put them in a strainer and dip them in boiling water, until the gills curl. The oysters, after this heat treatment, have shrunk slightly, are plump instead of flat, and the flesh has become firm in texture. They are now ready for processing.

Soak them in the Basic Fish Brine. Average-size oysters should be brined for 30 minutes; extra-large ones may have 40 to 45 minutes. Then rinse briefly in fresh water, and place on oiled racks or oiled sheets of aluminum foil, pierced with many small holes, until they are completely dry.

Begin smoking at 75° to 85°F. for about 30 minutes, then raise the temperature to 150°F. and smoke until the gills look dried. This usually takes about another 20 to 30 minutes. Towards the end of this time, take one oyster out and taste it. Watch closely to see that they are not overdone.

The oysters taste good, straight from the smoke oven. They may be given the oil treatment described above for octopus. After oiling, leave them for a few hours before serving, and they will develop a superlative flavor.

## Clams

Clams are treated exactly the same as oysters, including the technique for removing them from the shells.

## Scallops, Mussels

Treat the same as oysters.

## Squid

Cut open the body and remove the digestive organs. Place in boiling water to firm the flesh, then cut into small pieces or leave whole.

Cure in octopus brine for 45 to 60 minutes, then smoke the chunks just as if they were oysters.

## Shrimp, Prawns, Crayfish (Crawfish)

These three species are processed identically, so the instructions given for one can be applied to all.

Peel the shrimp while raw, and put into Basic Fish Brine. The time of brining will vary with size, from 15 to 45 minutes. Remove from brine, rinse lightly in fresh water, and put on racks or perforated sheets of aluminum foil, to dry.

Begin smoking at 85°F. After about 15 minutes, increase the temperature gradually to 135°F.

After 60 to 90 minutes, the shrimp should have taken on a rich amber color. Taste one of medium size to see if it is done. Remove them, or prolong the smoking a little, accordingly.

They are delicious hot or cold. They may be given the oil treatment already described for octopus.

## BRINE CURE—COLD SMOKING

Prepare the fish as already described by cleaning, gutting and, if desired, by cutting into fillets or chunks. Then immerse the fish in Basic Fish Brine for a time proportional to the weight, as specified by the table earlier in this chapter.

Remove from the brine and rinse briefly in fresh water. Hang in a cool airy place for 3 hours or longer if necessary, until the surface is completely dry.

Hang the fish, or place on racks, in the smoke oven. Keep the temperature between 70° and 85°F. and use a fairly light smoke. In prolonged cold-smoking, it is not essential that smoke be generated all the time. At night, for example, it does not matter if the hardwood is all consumed, or if the fire goes out. Simply compensate for the lost time when calculating the total smoking period.

The time required for cold smoking depends upon the time that the fish is to be kept. The following table will give a rough guide.

| Smoking Time | Keeping Time |
|---|---|
| 24 hours | 2 weeks |
| 2 days | 4 weeks |
| 3 days | 2 months |
| 4 days | 4 months |
| 5 days | 6 months |
| 1 week | 1 year |
| 2 weeks | 3 years |

These times assume a steady volume of smoke and uniform oven temperature.

Well-smoked fish will keep for some time at room temperature, but for best preservation, each fish or piece should be separately wrapped in waxed paper or aluminum foil and refrigerated at 35° F. During long storage, inspect one of the fish occasionally for signs of deterioration. A slight, localized growth of mold does not mean that the whole fish is bad. It can be scraped or cut off before the fish is used.

Cold-smoked fish may be eaten as it is. It can be heated before serving, or it can be used as an ingredient in various recipes. Some such recipes are given later in this chapter.

## Kippered Herring

"Kipper" is derived from an Anglo-Saxon word meaning the reddish color of a male salmon at spawning time. "Kippering" presumably used to mean processing other fish to make them look somewhat like smoked salmon. The word now has different meanings in different places; one can buy kippered salmon, kippered herring, kippered halibut, canned kippered snacks, and so on. Some of these "kippered" products are dyed to a reddish color. Others are not.

The method described next certainly cannot claim to be the one and only authentic kippered herring process, however, it does yield a very tasty product.

First, split the herring down the back, leaving the two halves connected by the belly skin. Remove the guts, gills and head, and leave the tail attached. Then soak for 30 minutes in Basic Fish Brine.

This next stage is optional. Many people prefer the natural, silvery color of herrings. However, if a red color is desired, dip the fish for 15 seconds in kipper color, prepared as described earlier for kippered salmon.

Hang up till completely dry. Then smoke at 85° F. for 12 hours. Take care that the fish is hung up or laid out so that the smoke gets to every part of its surface.

This will keep under refrigeration for at least 2 weeks. It is ready to eat without further preparation, but some people like to fry, boil or steam before serving.

## DRY CURE PROCESS

In this process the salt and other seasonings are applied, not in a brine, but in dry form, directly to the surface of the fish.

### Dry Cure, Hot Smoke

This technique will serve for most kinds of fish. Here are the steps.

1. Clean, gut and split the fish. Big fish may be divided into fillets or chunks. Chill the fish to 35°F. and wipe it dry.

2. Take the Dry Cure Mixture or Spiced Dry Cure Mixture and place the well-mixed ingredients in a shallow pan or dish. Place the clean, chilled fish in the pan and rub the mixture lightly into the flesh; turn over and rub the mixture into the other side. Remove carefully so that some of the mixture adheres to the surface of the fish. To ensure good penetration of the mixture, thick pieces of fish—1 inch or more—should be scored lengthwise with a sharp knife, about three quarters through, and the cuts two inches apart. The ingredients should be well rubbed into the score cuts.

3. Lay the fish in a pan or dish and keep at 35°F. for about 8 hours.

4. Rinse briefly in fresh water and hang up in a cool, airy place for 3 hours, or until the surface is completely dry.

5. Begin smoking at 75° to 85°F. for 30 to 60 minutes, to give ample absorption of the smoke flavor. Raise oven temperature to 150°F. and maintain there till fish is cooked, as revealed by flaking under pressure, or till a meat thermometer in the center of a thick piece shows 140°F.

### A Special Cure for Salmon

Proceed exactly as described above, except that to the standard Dry Cure mixture is added a few ounces of rum. This will be absorbed by the fish with the other ingredients, and will give an unusual, rich flavor to the finished product. Artificial rum flavoring may be substituted.

### Hawaiian Style Salmon

When applying the dry cure, rub the salmon thoroughly with some pineapple slices. Leave the pineapple in contact with the fish throughout the eight-hour curing period. Alternatively, lay crushed pineapple on and around the fish while it is curing.

### Dry Cure, Cold Smoke

The standard method for most kinds of fish is to proceed through steps 1 to 4 exactly as described under the Dry Cure Hot Smoke method.

Then smoke at a temperature between 70° and 85°F. from 24 hours to 2 weeks, depending on the time for which the fish is to be kept. Store as described under Brine Cure, Cold Smoking.

### Red Herring

The old-fashioned red herring was very heavily salted, and given a lengthy cold-smoking, so that it would keep for a long time even in warm storage conditions. Here is a modern method.

Clean and gut the herring, leaving the head on. Then apply the standard Dry Cure mixture. Leave the herring to cure for 7 days at 35°F., applying more of the Dry Cure mixture when the first application has all been absorbed.

Rinse in fresh water and hang up to dry. The herring now is ready to smoke at 70° to 85°F. for one week. Use plenty of smoke to produce the desired rich reddish color and strong spicy flavor.

This will keep for a year under refrigeration. It can be eaten without further cooking or, if preferred, may be steamed, fried or grilled. It makes exceptionally tasty eating.

### Yarmouth Bloater

Take a big herring, clean and scale the outside, but *do not* remove the guts, head or tail. This is an exception to the general rule that fish must be gutted before processing.

Apply the standard Dry Cure mixture and keep at 35°F. for 12 hours. Then cold-smoke at a temperature between 70° and 85°F. for 3 or 4 hours. The aim is to give the fish only a very mild smoke flavor. Smoking should be stopped before the skin turns brown.

The bloater may be kept a day or two under refrigeration, but no more. It is best fried or grilled and eaten promptly.

Because of its perishable nature, the bloater is almost unobtainable commercially nowadays.

## BAKING IN THE SMOKE OVEN

Fish may be baked in the smoke oven without any preliminary brining or dry curing. Prepare the fish just as if it was to be baked in an ordinary stove. Heat the oven to 200° to 225°F. and make a medium density of smoke. Keep the fish uncovered to pick up the smoke flavor. Baking time may be the same as, or a little longer than, that for the same food in a regular oven.

## TASTY FISH DISHES

Smoked fish is delicious served as it comes from the oven, whole, halved, in fillets or chunks, but it can also be used as the basic material for many tasty dishes, all of them quite easy to prepare. Here are some recipes.

### Smoked Fish Cakes

1 lb. smoked fish, flaked
½ cup chopped onion
2 tablespoons melted fat or oil
2 cups cold mashed potatoes
¼ cup chopped parsley
1 egg, beaten
Dash of pepper
½ cup dry breadcrumbs

Cook onion in fat until tender. Then combine all ingredients except crumbs, and shape the mixture into cakes. Next, roll the cakes in the breadcrumbs.

Fry in hot fat at moderate heat for 3 or 4 minutes, until one side is brown. Turn carefully and fry till the other side is brown.

Remove from the pan and drain on absorbent paper.

This recipe serves six. These fish cakes can, if desired, be served as fishburgers, in warmed, buttered buns, with lemon wedges on the side.

### Smoked Fish Chowder

1¼ lbs. smoked fish, flaked
1 cup cooked tomatoes
1 small onion, finely chopped
2 cups water
3 cups milk
¼ cup flour
1½ teaspoons Basic Seasoning

Simmer the smoked fish, tomatoes, onion and water for 20

minutes. In a separate pot, make thickening by combining the flour, milk and seasoning. Cook until thickened, stirring constantly.

When ready, mix the thickening with the smoked fish mixture, and serve at once.

## Smoked Shrimp Cheddar Casserole

2 cups smoked shrimp
1½ cups sharp cheddar cheese, grated
2 cups sliced fresh mushrooms
½ cup green onion, chopped
½ lb. cooked salad-type macaroni
1 pint sour cream
1 tablespoon curry powder
1 tablespoon onion powder
1 tablespoon lemon juice
6 tablespoons butter

Sauté the mushrooms in the butter; when nearly done, add the curry powder and onion powder. Blend the lemon juice, sour cream and 1 cup of the grated cheese; add the onions and shrimp.

Make sure the macaroni is well drained, then add the cooked mushrooms and the sour cream mixture, and toss lightly.

Heap in a 1½ quart casserole, sprinkle with the remaining cheese, and bake at 375° F. for 25 to 30 minutes.

## Smoked Fish Sandwich Spread

2 cups smoked fish, finely flaked
1 cup crushed pineapple, well drained
mayonnaise

Mix the fish and pineapple and add just enough mayonnaise to produce a spread of the desired consistency.

Spread between bread slices buttered on the *outer* sides. Grill until the bread is well browned.

If desired, a slice of sharp cheese may be placed, along with the spread, between the bread slices before they are grilled.

## Smoked Fish and Cheese Dip

1½ cups smoked fish, flaked
6 ounces cream cheese
1 clove garlic, finely minced
3 tablespoons minced onion
¼ teaspoon salt
2 tablespoons Worcestershire sauce
1 tablespoon lemon juice
Strips of pimento

Mash the smoked fish with the cheese and blend in the seasonings. Chill for several hours, to give the flavors time to blend.

Garnish with the pimento strips before serving. Use as a dip for crackers, potato chips or corn chips. Makes about 2¼ cups.

## Special Smoked Fish Sandwich

Proceed as with the recipe for Sleight's Special Beef Sandwich in Chapter 4, but substitute for the smoked beef 2 tablespoons finely flaked smoked fish.

CHAPTER 8

# Sausages

SAUSAGE HAS BEEN AN IMPORTANT meat staple for more than five thousand years. Many countries—even many individual cities—have produced their special varieties. This chapter gives instructions for making, from butcher's meat and from wild game, a number of sausages in which smoking is important for enhanced flavor or for improved keeping qualities.

## SUMMER OR WINTER?

It was formerly believed, indeed, some writers still assert, that certain types of sausages could be made only in winter. Undoubtedly, the many so-called "winter sausages" were originally made and consumed in winter because they would not keep in hot weather. Yet nowadays commercial plants make winter sausage all year round, and anyone can do the same wherever he lives, by using a refrigerator.

Summer sausage, on the other hand, is so called because it will keep. It originally offered a means of preserving winter-killed meat in the form of hard sausages right on through spring and summer without spoilage. This problem of preserving meat in hot weather was more severe in the Mediterranean area than in the cooler countries of northern Europe, so the Mediterranean countries have produced the most varieties of summer sausage.

## GRINDERS

The grinder is an essential piece of equipment for sausage making, although the name "grinder" is really a misnomer. The cutters in the machine should be very sharp, so that it slices and chops the meat rather than grinding or crushing it. The output of the machine should consist of clean-cut pieces, no matter how small they are. If the meat comes out mashed into pulp it will not make good sausages.

A butcher supply house where the machine was purchased has facilities for properly sharpening the grinder blades if they get dull. A rather less satisfactory method that can be used at home is to lay the blade flat on a sharpening-stone and slide it back and forth until the cutting edges are keen.

It is desirable to have several different cutting plates for the machine, to give various degrees of fineness in the cutting. Plates with holes of $3/8$ inch, $3/16$ inch and $1/8$ inch are useful. The $3/16$ cutting plate, used alone, will give a medium-coarse texture to the sausage. For a fine texture, grind with two different plates. On the first cut, use the $3/8$ inch plate; on the second cut, the $1/8$ inch plate.

To force the meat down into the machine, some people use their fingers, but it is safer and more sanitary to use the proper tool for the job, a cylindrical plunger of wood or plastic called a stomper.

Hand grinders will serve for making small quantities of sausage. For bigger-scale production there are powered models of various sizes, ranging from the small ones designed for domestic use up to the large commercial grinders.

A handyman can convert a manually-operated grinder to power drive with an old motor from a washer or dryer and a little ingenuity. It may be necessary to try a few different sizes of pulleys on the grinder or the motor to get just the right speed, but a few experiments will show how it can be done.

## STUFFERS

Stuffing attachments in the form of spouts ½″ or ¾″ diameter can be fitted on the output end of some meat grinders. For this purpose the cutters and plate are removed. Such an attachment will be adequate for small-scale production. But to make large quantities of sausages, a separate sausage stuffer is desirable. This machine has a big cylinder (different sizes hold 12, 18 or 24 lbs. of ground meat) and a piston driven by a powerful rack-and-pinion movement to force the meat out of the spout. These machines have several sizes of spouts, up to 1″ diameter.

## CASINGS

Several kinds of sausage casings are available. Natural casings are made from sheep, pig and beef intestines. When stuffed, they yield a sausage from 1″ to 4″ diameter. They come in lengths of several feet. They are expensive, and can cost 20 to 25 cents for each pound of meat that is put into them. They have in the past had one major advantage—they are edible.

Sheep and hog casings are available in a brine package, or salted dry. Beef casings are sold only in brine. Most people who choose natural casings prefer the sheep or hog casings.

The natural casings—for pork or wild game breakfast links—are packaged 1 hank per bag. In size $^{18}/_{20}$, one hank stuffs approximately 40 lbs. of sausage. In size $^{20}/_{22}$, one hank stuffs approximately 50 lbs. of sausage.

Natural casings, brined or dry salted, should be kept refrigerated or frozen. Even in the freezer, the brine will not turn to ice, so any amount may be taken out as required.

There is now available an *edible* plastic casing in 18mm to 32mm sizes, at about the same price as natural casings. This material can be kept indefinitely without brining or refrigeration. There is, however, one necessary precaution in stuffing; these casings must be filled from a straight, parallel-sided spout, not from the tapered spout commonly used with natural casings. There is not much likelihood that natural casings will come down in price, but there may be further developments and possibly price reductions, with the edible plastic casings.

Inedible plastic casings, for big sausages, are available in 2″ to 6″ diameter, and from 24″ to 36″ in length. They are not too satisfactory for home use because as the sausage is smoked and aged, the meat shrinks, but the casing does not; so the casing becomes loose-fitting and wrinkled. If these casings are used, friends and guests may need to be reminded that they are not meant to be eaten.

For big sausages, the most desirable casing is plain unbleached muslin. Here are instructions for making an 18″ casing, to produce a finished sausage about 15″ long.

First, tear unbleached muslin into strips 8″ × 18″. Fold in half lengthwise and press with a medium-hot iron.

The selvage edge of the cloth is to be left for the opening. At the other end of the folded cloth, take a cup, tumbler, or other round object about 3½″ diameter and, using it as a template, make a semi-circular mark with a soft pencil near the end of the cloth. The mark should at no point come nearer than ¼″ to the end of the cloth.

Beginning at the folded edge, sew around the semi-circular mark, and continue to sew in a straight line up the torn edge, keeping the stitches at least ¼″ in from the edge. The folded strip of cloth is now converted into a tube open at one end.

With pinking shears, trim around the sewn end and edge. This removes loose threads that would otherwise adhere to the sausage when the casing is eventually removed. But take care not to pink too close to the stitches, or the casing may burst under the pressure of stuffing.

Turn the casing inside-out, and it is ready to use.

It is often desirable to make several different sizes of casings for one batch of sausages. For example, to provide a light snack for three or four people, a 15″ sausage is too much. If only half of it is served, the rest may dry out before the next time it is used. So some casings might well be cut about 9″ or 12″ in length.

Many smoke ovens have no room to hang sausages longer than 15″. With such an oven, if larger sausages are required, make them thicker. Tear the muslin strip wider—9″ or 10″.

## USING SAUSAGE CASINGS

### Preparing the Casings

Natural casings: dry salted casings must be thoroughly washed before use. The brine-packed casings may be used as they are.

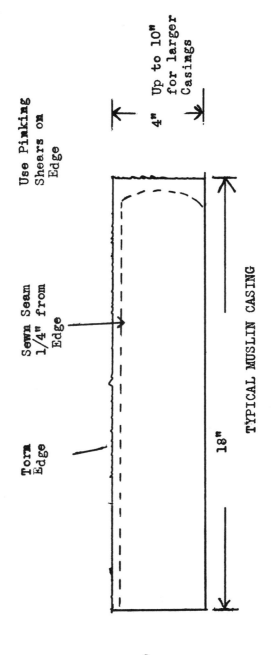

Use Pinking
Shears on
Edge

4" Up to 10"
for larger
Casings

Sewn Seam
1/4" from
Edge

Torn
Edge

18"

TYPICAL MUSLIN CASING

Selvage
Edge

Plastic casings: soak 2 or 3 minutes in water before use.

Muslin casings: soak in water and wring out, so that they are damp when filled with meat.

## Before Stuffing

Slip the casing over the spout of the stuffer. Run the stuffer briefly until a little meat is extruded from the end of the spout.

If the meat is too dry, it will not come out easily; then some water or wine should be added and well mixed in with the meat, to get a more fluid consistency that will work smoothly through the stuffer spout. A little experience will lead to attaining the right consistency the first time.

But the first section of meat is still projecting from the spout. So, with natural or plastic casings, tie the end of the casing with a piece of string to enclose this meat. The end of the muslin casing, of course, is already sewed up. Take care to avoid air pockets at this point; the end of the sausage should be completely filled with meat. If air is left entrapped here, there is risk of decay.

## Stuffing

Turn the crank, or switch on the motor to start the stuffer running. As meat is expelled from the spout, see that the casing is completely filled, with no air-pockets anywhere along its length. Hold one hand just under the spout, so that the newly-formed sausage slides gently over it. This avoids the risk of having the sausage kink as it comes off the spout. Such kinks would be likely to form air-pockets.

For link-type sausages, use natural or edible plastic casings; muslin is not suitable for such a small sausage.

The larger casings offer little difficulty in stuffing, neither do the link-size edible plastic casings. Breakfast sausages in sheep casings do require careful handling. The natural casings vary in strength according to the time of year the sheep was butchered, and to what its diet had been. But here are some hints that will help solve the problem.

Excess pressure while filling may burst the casing. So make the meat more moist for these casings than for plastic or muslin, so that it will come more easily from the spout. Also let the casing slip fairly easily from the spout so that there is never any great resistance or tension.

Excess pressure may also burst the casings at the moment they are twisted into links. If the links do not form easily on twisting, ease up further on the pressure of the meat. The ideal is that, after twisting, each link should be just nicely plump and filled with meat, but not unduly strained.

### Closing

When the casing is full, tie the end with a string so tightly that a little meat is forced out of the end. This, again, tends to exclude air. Use plenty of strong string so that, after tying, enough string is left to form a loop for hanging the sausage during refrigeration, smoking and storage.

### Smoking

In a long smoking process the meat, through dehydration, will shrink by as much as half its original weight. Natural casings and muslin will shrink with the meat. Plastic, as mentioned earlier, does not shrink.

With muslin casings, the color-change will show how the smoking is proceeding. When the muslin is a rich amber color, the sausage will usually be sufficiently smoked.

## EXPERIMENTATION

Many readers, after gaining some experience with the sausage recipes offered here, will wish to create new, original recipes. Here is an economical way to proceed.

Do not risk a whole batch of meat on an experiment that may or may not succeed. Instead, when making a batch from a well-tried recipe, hold back a pound or two of meat and experiment with that. Here are some of the variables that can be tried.

Different combinations of meats.

Different ingredients or different times for the preliminary brine cure or dry cure.

Different seasonings, wines or other flavoring ingredients added after the cure.

Different grinding procedures—coarser, finer.

Different times, temperatures or hardwoods for smoking.

There is no need to wait until after the smoking to test a new recipe. When the sausage is ready to go into the smoke oven, cook a few slices in the frying pan. If it tastes good at this stage, it will taste even better after smoking. If it is not satisfactory at this stage, there is still a chance to do something about it in the way of altering the seasoning content, regrinding, etc., before the smoking begins.

## SUMMER SAUSAGE

This excellent sausage can be made in many ways. One basic recipe is described first; following this are some suggestions for making different varieties.

### Ingredients

12 lbs. lean beef
8 lbs. pork*
3 ozs. white pepper
1 oz. salt
1 tablespoon powdered garlic
½ oz. whole black peppers
⅓ oz. mustard seed
1 oz. coriander seed
40 fluid ounces dry red wine

*The pork should contain an average amount of fat. Or, use 4 lbs. lean pork and 4 lbs. fat. Shoulder butts are a good cut. The shoulder blades can easily be trimmed out with a sharp boning knife. If the butt is very lean, add some pork or beef fat to get the optimum consistency. Pork shoulder can be used, but this entails more trimming and more waste.

### Curing the Beef

Cut the beef into cubes approximately 2" x 2" x 2". Place the cubes in a crock of Sweet Pickle Brine or some equivalent ready-packaged brine cure. Weight the meat down so that it stays submerged. Keep at 35°F. for 8 to 12 days. Overhaul every fourth day, thoroughly stirring up the pickle each time. Remove from the brine, rinse quickly in cold water and lay out to dry on wire mesh racks or on sheets of aluminum foil pierced with drainage holes, in a refrigerator for 24 hours.

## Mixing the Ingredients

When the beef is thoroughly dry, cut the pork up into chunks small enough to go into the meat grinder. Put the pork and the cured beef in a large pan. Add the white pepper, salt and garlic powder and mix thoroughly. The whole black peppers, mustard seed and coriander seed are *not* added at this stage; they would be cracked open by the subsequent grinding.

## Grinding

For a medium-coarse texture, put the mixed ingredients twice through the grinder with a ³⁄₁₆″ plate. For a fine texture, put once through a ³⁄₈″ plate and once through a ⅛″ plate.

## Final Seasoning

In a large pan add the other seasonings and the wine to the ground meat, and mix thoroughly. Put the pan in the refrigerator and let it stand for at least 2 days.

## Stuffing

Cut muslin for casings about 8″ × 18″. This will yield sausages about 2″ in diameter when folded and sewn. Wet the cases, stuff as full as possible, and tie off tightly with strong string.

## Hanging

Hang the stuffed sausages in the refrigerator at about 35°F. for at least 2 days. S-hooks made of malleable wire will be handy for hanging the sausages from the refrigerator racks.

## Smoking

Smoke in a fairly cool oven—85° to 95°F.—until the muslin cases are a rich, dark brown. This should take 12 to 15 hours.

## Maturing

Remove from the smoke oven and hang in the refrigerator at 35°F. for at least 3 weeks. After smoking and maturing, these sausages which originally weighed about 2½ lbs. each, will be reduced to about 1 lb. each. This weight reduction is entirely due to dehydration; not a scrap of nutritive value has been lost. The finished sausages are a highly concentrated, delicious food.

### Storing

At this stage, the sausages may be kept in refrigeration, although this is not essential. They will keep indefinitely in any cool dry place. If mold appears on the casings, it is harmless. Simply wipe it off with a cloth dampened in vinegar. Or, if the sausage is about to be eaten, simply peel off the mold-specked casing and throw it away. The meat inside is perfectly sound.

### Serving

Remove the casing before serving. This sausage can be sliced very thin and eaten as it is, without any cooking. Dice and mix with scrambled eggs or potato salad. Mince and mix with a favorite filling for devilled (stuffed) eggs. Slice and serve on cocktail crackers, spread with different cheeses.

### Further Tips

Go slow! The making of summer sausage should not be hurried. The times mentioned above for final seasoning, hanging and maturing are minima. Longer times will give even better results. Much of the flavor of good summer sausage comes from the gradual blending of many different flavors and aromas. Time for this process is just as important as is time in the making of good wines.

### Variations

The basic beef-and-pork recipe just given can be varied considerably. The amount of pork should not be changed, but for the beef can be substituted any other red meat, domestic or wild—venison, moose, elk, bear, etc.—or any combination of different red meats to make up the weight of 12 lbs.

## SUMMER SAUSAGE—DRY CURE

If the meat is already ground when purchased, the brine cure is not suitable; this dry cure technique should be used instead. One important point is that the dry cure works faster than the equivalent brine cure, so saves a week to ten days in total processing time. This can be useful in making sausages to a deadline.

### Ingredients

    12 lbs. lean beef
     8 lbs. pork
    10 oz. Dry Cure For Meat
     1 oz. salt
     3 ozs. white pepper
     1 tablespoon powdered garlic
     ½ oz. whole black peppers
     ⅓ oz. mustard seed
     1 oz. coriander seed
    40 fluid ounces dry red wine

### Mixing the Ingredients

If the meat is not already ground, cut it in pieces small enough to go into the grinder. Mix the two meats together with the Dry Cure, white pepper and garlic powder, and put through the grinder. For a medium-coarse texture, put the mixed ingredients twice through a 3/16″ plate. For a fine texture, put once through a ⅜″ plate and once through a ⅛″ plate.

If the meat is already ground, mix it thoroughly with the Dry Cure, white pepper and garlic powder, then put it once through the grinder.

### Curing, Final Seasoning, Etc.

Spread out the meat in a shallow pan and refrigerate at 40°F. for 3 or 4 days. Add the other seasonings and the wine, and mix thoroughly. Spread out as before and refrigerate at 40°F. for another 1 or 2 days.

For stuffing, hanging, smoking, maturing, storage and serving, follow the instructions for the brine-cure summer sausage. With this, as with the brine-cure sausage, better results will follow if more time is allowed for seasoning, hanging and maturing.

The same red meats mentioned under the brine cure may equally well be substituted for beef with the dry cure.

### SALAMI

For this sausage, the meat requires no preliminary curing; therefore salami can be made more quickly than summer sausage.

## Ingredients

> 10 lbs. pork
> 10 lbs. lean beef
> 1½ lbs. onions
> 1 tablespoon powdered garlic
> 8 ozs. salt
> 4 teaspoons black pepper
> 4 teaspoons white pepper
> 40 fluid ounces dry red wine (optional)

## Mixing and Grinding

Dice the onions and cut the meat into chunks small enough to go into the meat grinder. Mix all ingredients except the wine in a large pan.

For a medium-coarse texture, put the mixture twice through the grinder with a ³⁄₁₆″ plate. For a fine texture, put once through a ³⁄₈″ and once through a ⅛″ plate.

## Seasoning, Stuffing and Hanging

Add the wine and mix thoroughly in a large pan. Put the pan in the refrigerator and let it stand 2 days at 35°F.

Cut muslin for cases about 8″ × 18″ to yield, when folded, sewn and stuffed, a sausage about 2″ diameter. Wet the cases, stuff as full as possible, and tie off tightly with strong string.

Hang the stuffed sausages in a refrigerator at 35°F. for 2 days.

## Smoking

Smoke in a fairly cool oven—85° to 95°F.—until the muslin cases are a rich, dark brown. This should take 12 to 15 hours.

## Storage and Serving

This sausage will keep under refrigeration as long as, but no longer than any other uncured, smoked meat, say 3 or 4 weeks. For longer storage, salami should be frozen. Wrapped closely in aluminum foil, or put in plastic bags, and frozen at 0°F., it will keep in perfect condition for a year or more.

This sausage must be thoroughly cooked before it is eaten. To serve, remove casing, cut in thick slices, and fry.

## Maintaining Freshness

Since the meats are not cured, it is particularly important that they be chilled to 35°F. before mixing begins, and kept near that temperature throughout the processing. Mixing and grinding should be done quickly and, if possible, in a cool place. The grinding process itself tends to warm the meat. So between the first and second grindings, it is a good precaution to put the meat back in the refrigerator until it is thoroughly chilled again.

## Variations

As with summer sausage, other red meats, singly or in combination, can be substituted for the beef.

## BREAKFAST SAUSAGE

    25 lbs. pork
     8 ozs. Basic Seasoning
     2 tablespoons sage
     1 tablespoon thyme
    40 fluid ounces of some favorite wine

## Ingredients, Grinding and Seasoning

Cut the pork up into chunks small enough to go into the meat grinder. Add the seasonings and mix thoroughly. In grinding, put twice through a ³/₁₆″ plate. Add the wine, mix well in a large pan, and let it stand in the refrigerator at 35°F. for 24 hours.

## Stuffing and Smoking

Use natural lamb casings; rinse in water before use. As the casing fills, twist it into links about 4 inches long. For smoking, lay the links on racks (if hung up, they will untwist) and smoke at 85° to 90°F. until the casings are a rich amber color.

## Storing and Serving

Refrigerate at 35°F. for up to 3 weeks; or wrap in plastic bags and freeze at 0°F. for up to 6 months. Serve fried with potatoes, eggs, etc.

## Other Notes

If desired, commercially-packaged pork sausage seasoning may be substituted for the seasonings here listed. Use about 8 ozs. for each 25 lbs. of meat.

The same recipe may be stuffed into muslin cases, 2½″ diameter, and cut into slices for cooking.

A delicious sausage results from taking equal weights of lamb and pork, seasoned and smoked just like the pure pork.

Beef will make a good breakfast sausage, alone, or mixed with pork.

Any wild game meat can be used, alone or with pork, and processed in the same way.

## SPECIAL SAUSAGE SANDWICH

Refer back to Sleight's Special Beef Sandwich recipe in Chapter 4. A good sandwich can be made by substituting for the beef a similar quantity of sausage, thinly sliced or diced. Other ingredients, and processing, are the same.

# CHAPTER 9

# Miscellaneous Delicacies

THERE ARE SEVERAL SMOKED FOODS that do not fit in any of the preceding chapters. This chapter describes some such items.

## SMOKED CHEESE

Almost any cheese may be given a gentle smoking to enhance its flavor. Soft cheeses will absorb the smoke more readily than the firmer varieties. In addition to the well-known domestic cheeses, there are some foreign ones that take particularly well to smoking. From Norway—Norvegia and Jarlsberg; from Finland—Lappi; from Denmark—Dofo Tybo; and from Austria—Fortina. Here are some hints for successful smoking of cheese.

From a short exposure to very heavy smoke, cheese may pick up a slightly sooty flavor, so a light smoke and a somewhat longer application is desirable. Two hours of light smoke is a fair average.

Low temperature—especially with the softer cheeses—is essential. The oven should certainly not get above 80°F. Below 75°F. will be better.

To give maximum absorption of smoke, the cheese should preferably be in fairly thin slabs—not thicker than 1½ inches or cubes 1 inch by 1 inch. Any rind, peel, wax coating, or other protective layer should be removed before smoking begins.

The cheese will necessarily lose some weight, will shrink a little, and become somewhat firmer in texture during smoking. This is merely the result of partial dehydration, and does not indicate any loss of nutriment.

After smoking, cheese should be wrapped again as it was before, and kept under refrigeration. However, it will not yield its finest flavor if it is eaten cold. Remove it from the refrigerator an hour or two before it is required, and give it time to warm up to room temperature.

One interesting point about smoked cheese, it remains fresh and free from any sign of mold or decay much longer than a similar unsmoked cheese, even if kept at room temperature.

## SMOKED NUTS

Most kinds of nuts can be successfully smoked—almonds, walnuts, peanuts, cashews, Brazil nuts, canned mixed nuts, roast chestnuts, etc.

Nuts will fall through the typical oven rack, so they are spread out on a fine screen, or on a sheet of aluminum foil pierced with many holes.

Smoke at 75° to 85°F. for 2 to 3 hours. Use a fairly light smoke. Like cheese, nuts cannot stand a heavy smoke. In a dense smoke they will acquire an unpleasant burned, sooty flavor.

As for salt, this is a matter for individual taste. Some people like salt on certain nuts; others do not.

To apply salt before smoking, soak small nuts for a few minutes in brine, and let them drain before going into the smoke oven. Alternatively, they can be shaken up with dry salt in a plastic bag. Big nuts, like Brazils and chestnuts, can be individually dipped in salt as they are eaten.

For use with nuts, smoked salt gives an additional zest to the final flavor.

## SMOKED SEEDS

Pumpkin and sunflower seeds, commonly eaten as snacks, can be given a new flavor by smoking. Both kinds are processed alike. First, soak the seeds overnight in a saturated salt solution.

Drain the seeds and spread them on a fine wire screen, or on a sheet of foil pierced with many holes.

Smoke the seeds for 1 hour at about 85°F., then hotsmoke at 200° to 225°F. for 1 hour, or until the seeds are thoroughly dry.

For an interesting flavor variant, add Worcestershire sauce to the brine, 2 teaspoons to each quart.

## SMOKED EGGS

Hard boil the eggs. Very fresh eggs are hard to peel after boiling, so use eggs that are several days old. Begin with a pan of cool water, about the same temperature as the eggs. Add 1 tablespoon of vinegar for each quart of water. Put the eggs in and turn on the heat. The moment the water begins to boil, remove the pan from the heat. *Do not let the water come to a rolling boil.* Leave the eggs in the slowly cooling water for 15 minutes, then cool and peel. They may be left whole or sliced with an egg slicer.

Place the whole or sliced eggs on a screen and smoke about 85°F. until they are a rich amber color. For extra flavor, sprinkle with Basic Seasoning before smoking, and/or oil like oysters after smoking.

Serve as devilled eggs, sliced, spread with salad dressing, sprinkled with paprika for hors d'oeuvres, or diced for potato salad.

## SMOKED FROG'S LEGS

Apply Basic Seasoning liberally. Cold-smoke at 75° to 85°F. for about 1 hour, or until the meat takes on a rich, golden color. Then raise the oven temperature to 225° to 250° F. and roast until done, basting carefully with vegetable oil or butter.

For a markedly different flavor, marinate before smoking. Use the marinade recommended for chicken livers, hearts and gizzards in Chapter 5, with a dry white wine. Marinate 2 hours, then smoke as described above.

## SMOKED BLUEBERRIES

Pacific Coast Indians used to smoke-dry blueberries for winter use. They may be successfully processed in an ordinary smoke oven.

Spread the blueberries on a fine wire screen and cold-smoke at 75° to 85°F. until they are partly dehydrated. The skins become wrinkled, and they look somewhat like dried currants.

Keep in a covered—though not airtight—jar or dish under refrigeration.

The smoked berries make a very tasty dessert served with ice cream or sherbet.

## GARLIC BREAD

Bread prepared by this recipe is unequalled for serving with smoked meats of all kinds.

    1 long, thin loaf unsliced French bread
    4 ozs. butter
    5 ozs. sharp spreadable cheese,
      old American or Roquefort
    1 teaspoon garlic powder (more or less, to taste)

Soften the butter and cheese. Thoroughly mix with the garlic powder.

Cut the bread into slices ½″ to ¾″ thick.

Part the slices, and spread with the butter-cheese-garlic mixture. It is not enough to put a dot in the middle of each slice; cover the slices all over, right to the edges.

Wrap closely in aluminum foil, folding and crimping the edges carefully to make a near-airtight package. Heat in the smoke oven or kitchen oven at 250° for 30 minutes.

Before serving, open up the foil. When that is done, turn the foil up around the sides to form a boat-shaped receptacle that will keep the bread warm.

# CHAPTER 10

# Canning
# Smoked Food

IT MAY SOMETIMES BE DESIRABLE to preserve a batch of smoked food beyond the time it could be kept under refrigeration. For this purpose, canning is the best technique. Canning is also a practical and pleasing way to package smoked foods for use as gifts.

## CANNING TECHNIQUES

Innumerable books and pamphlets from commercial publishers, government departments, and from makers of canning equipment, describe the techniques of canning, so there is no need to give detailed instructions here. It will suffice to mention several points specially relevant to the canning of smoked foods.

### Sterilization

It would be wrong and dangerous to assume that the smoking process in any way reduces the need for thorough sterilization of the food and of the cans or jars that contain it. All procedures and precautions should be exactly the same for smoked as for un-smoked food.

Sterilization in the oven, or by simply boiling in water, are not recommended. Far and away the best method is with the pressure cooker or canner. If manufacturer's instructions are closely followed, this method should present no difficulties.

For pint jars or cans packed with large pieces of meat or fish, process at 10 lbs. pressure for 75 minutes. For quart jars or cans, process at 10 lbs. for 90 minutes.

But remember that these formulas are valid only at or near sea level. At higher altitudes they may not provide complete steriliza-tion. So for each 2,000 feet above sea level, increase the pressure reading by 1 lb. but *do not* increase the time.

It makes no difference for this purpose whether the food has been hot-smoked or cold-smoked—whether it has been fully cooked, or merely flavored in the smoke oven. The same pressures and times must be used.

### Liquid Contents

In addition to the pieces of solid meat or fish, liquid must be added to the cans or jars.

For meat, broth or oil must be used. The broth is prepared by boiling spare pieces of the meat in water, skimming off any fat that rises to the top. The broth is poured, while still boiling, into the cans, to the level recommended in the instructions for the appara-tus being used—usually about 1 inch from the top. Vegetable oil may be used instead of the broth.

Each method has its advocates. Only by experiment can one find which better suits the tastes of one's family and friends. Here, as in many other aspects of food-smoking, it pays to keep careful records of what has been done with each batch of each kind of food. Then, months or years later, it will be possible to repeat ex-actly the method that produced a specially successful batch.

For smoked seafood, vegetable oil is the preferred liquid addi-tive. It may not always be necessary to add so much oil with fish as with a corresponding amount of meat. An oily fish such as sturgeon will give up much of its own oil during the sterilization process. About 2 tablespoons of oil will usually suffice for a pint jar. If too much fluid is used, some of it will escape, perhaps carrying minute particles of solid matter that will stick under the lid and prevent a proper airtight seal.

## Testing

It is a good precaution to examine cans and jars 24 hours after processing.

With jars, the lid should be slightly concave as a result of the partial vacuum within. Tapped at its center with a spoon, the lid should give a clear, metallic ring.

Can seams and seals should be visibly sound, the ends should be slightly concave.

If any cans or jars show signs of being leaky, play safe: either use the contents at once, or open them, repeat the entire canning procedure, and reseal in sound cans or jars.

After storage, and before use, again examine cans or jars for any sign of leakage or spoilage. A useful additional test, in a doubtful case, is to boil the food for 20 minutes in a *covered* pan; if, on lifting the lid, there arises the characteristic smell of bad meat or fish, throw the contents away without tasting.

These precautions are by no means needlessly fussy. They guard against a whole assortment of ills, especially botulism, a horrible and deadly form of food poisoning. Nevertheless, with reasonable care during and after canning, all danger can be eliminated, and much extra pleasure and economy can be obtained from the smoke oven.

# CHAPTER 11

# Big-Scale
# Production

THIS CHAPTER OFFERS SOME suggestions for adapting the previously-described techniques of smoke cookery and curing to big-scale production such as is required in holding large smoked-food parties or in supplying smoked foods to stores, hotels and banquet caterers.

## EQUIPMENT

A surprising amount of smoked food can be produced with a modest amount of equipment if that equipment is of the right kind and is used efficiently. Some detailed hints follow.

## Smoke Oven

There is no particular need for a big smoke oven. The author has catered to parties of 300 with an oven only 18″ x 18″ x 30″ internal measurements.

An electrically-heated oven with a thermostatically-controlled element would be a great advantage. It saves the operator's time because he does not have to keep checking the oven temperature.

A further refinement would be a time-switch that could be set, for example, to turn on the heating element at a predetermined time, and so change from cold-smoking to hot-smoking without the operator's attention, and then turn itself off after the correct period of hot-smoking. Such controls are normally fitted to modern kitchen stoves; they might just as well be utilized in smoke cookery.

## Refrigeration

Ample capacity for ordinary refrigeration and for freezing is absolutely essential for big-scale production. It allows advance preparation of many products. Then they need only be thawed or heated in time for delivery or consumption.

It also allows big-scale curing to proceed—several large crocks containing different meats, in different brines, to be removed for processing at different times.

A walk-in cooler and freezer would be ideal and, in regular commercial production, would pay for themselves. But a battery of three or four refrigerators plus a good freezer will serve as a fair substitute.

## Other Equipment

It is no use trying to skimp on equipment if large amounts of food are to be processed. Meat grinders and sausage stuffers must be big and amply powered. The right kind of knives, cleavers and other cutting tools must be available, and must be sharp. There must be plenty of jars, bowls, crocks and other containers for washing, brining, mixing, oiling and other processes.

Ample bench and shelf space is a great aid to easy, efficient operation. Though wooden cutting boards or blocks are adequate for home use, they may not fulfill the sanitary regulations if food is being processed commercially. For certain kinds of trade the law requires that meat and fish must be cut either on a stainless steel surface, or on one of the sanitary thermoplastic cutting boards that are now available in a wide range of thicknesses and areas. They are strong, long-lasting, easy to clean, and can conveniently be built in to a kitchen or work-room.

A big double-sink with abundant hot and cold water supply is just about essential.

A reserve stock of oven racks, trays and similar fittings can greatly speed operations.

## MATERIALS

For commercial production of smoked foods in large quantities, it is essential to arrange a wholesale supply of meats, fish and other ingredients. Without this, costs would be prohibitive.

## RECORDS

To build up a reputation, it is absolutely essential to produce foods of uniform quality. Wholesale or retail customers will soon become dissatisfied if foods vary continually in saltiness, color, spiciness, moisture or dryness, tenderness or toughness, and in keeping quality.

Careful record-keeping is the key to uniform quality. To know exactly what weights of meat or fish, what brining times, what smoking times and temperatures, what special seasonings, if any, were used on previous batches is the only way to repeat one's successes consistently, and to avoid the repetition of the occasional failure.

Experimentation, to be sure, is fascinating, and sometimes produces excellent results, but experiments should be conducted on a small scale, producing food for oneself and a few friends. Only well-tested recipes and techniques should be used on the big scale.

## ECONOMY

If food-smoking is undertaken as a part-time or full-time business, there can be no room for waste.

Brines, for instance, should be refreshed and re-used for several batches of food.

It costs money to heat the oven and keep it full of smoke, so the space should be well utilized either with full batches of one kind of food, or with smaller batches of different foods that require similar conditions of temperature and smoke density.

If different foodstuffs are smoked together, they must be properly arranged, so that one does not spoil the other. For example, fish and other seafoods should never be placed above meat or poultry; grease, protein juices or water dripping from the fish could spoil the poultry or meat flavor.

Poultry, on the other hand, can safely be placed *above* fish. Any fat that drips from the poultry is so bland that it will not spoil the flavor of the fish—indeed, it may be useful in helping to keep the fish moist.

Several different kinds of fish can be smoked at one time, especially if they are hung up side by side from rods or hooks.

If fish are being smoked on racks, begin by filling the bottom rack. When the dripping ceases, move this rack up and place a new batch of fish on the bottom. Proceed in the same way; as each bottom rack-full dries, move them all up one space and insert a new rack, until the oven is full. At this stage, the top rack will be ready to remove first. Take it out, move the others up, and put a fresh rack-full in at the bottom.

In this way, the oven is fully utilized; there is a steady output of fully-smoked fish, oysters, clams, etc. coming out, ready for further processing if required, and there is ample time to get each rack of unsmoked fish ready before it goes into the oven.

When one is smoking food as a business, time is money. It is inefficient and wasteful to fill the oven with food and stand watching it for two hours while it is being smoked. Operations can be scheduled so that while one batch of food is smoking, other tasks are carried out—cleaning fish, stuffing sausages, making brine, oiling oysters, etc.

## MENU PLANNING

To serve an elaborate smoked-food menu usually requires that some of the items be prepared in advance, while others are made ready as required. Here, for example, is the menu of a smoked-food party for 300 guests, and the planning chart which the author used to keep a different item of smoked food coming out of the kitchen every 15 minutes for five hours!

| Time | Food Served | Hot or Cold | Work To Do |
|------|-------------|-------------|------------|
| 2.00 | Elk Summer Sausage | Cold | Put spareribs in to warm. |
| 2.15 | Kokanie Salmon | Cold | — |
| 2.30 | Corned Beef Heart & Peruvian Style Beef Heart | Cold | — |
| 2.45 | Smelt | Cold | — |
| 3.00 | Spareribs | Hot | Put chicken in to warm. |
| 3.15 | Venison Jerky Chicken Liver Pate on Crackers | Cold | — |
| 3.30 | Lamb Summer Sausage Beef Kidney | Cold | Put elk in to warm. |
| 3.45 | Chicken | Hot | — |
| 4.00 | Octopus | Cold | Put rabbit & duck in to warm. |
| 4.15 | Elk Roast | Hot | Put turkey in to warm. |
| 4.30 | Shrimp & Prawns Bear Jerky | Cold | — |
| 4.45 | Rabbit & Duck | Hot | — |
| 5.00 | Oysters | Cold | — |
| 5.15 | Corned Bear Butter Clams | Cold | Put lamb in to warm. |
| 5.30 | Turkey | Hot | — |
| 5.45 | Salmon | Cold | Put venison in to warm. |
| 6.00 | Corned Buffalo | Cold | — |
| 6.15 | Lamb | Hot | — |
| 6.30 | Razor Clams | Cold | — |
| 6.45 | Venison | Hot | — |
| 7.00 | Sturgeon | Cold | — |

For rapid, sure-fire service, most of the food is fully smoked, or nearly finished, beforehand. The menu is arranged to separate the hot dishes by cold ones, so that there is ample time for warming each hot item. Some of the foods are warmed in the smoke oven, with a moderate smoke density, mainly to let guests see how it looks. (These foods had previously received most of the smoking they required.) Other foods are warmed in the regular kitchen oven.

With a smaller number of guests, it would be practical to do the complete smoking of certain foods on the day of the party or banquet, but then the foods would have to go into the oven sooner.

At a party of this kind, guests will consume an average of 1¼ lbs. each. The 300 people at the party described above ate 373 lbs. of meat and fish, although many of them were there only a part of the time!

## MARKETING

Anyone who wishes to make smoked foods for sale should check the local health laws and regulations. City and county health inspections are quite rigid in many areas. Then, if the products are to cross state lines, they may be subject to Federal regulations.

In many jurisdictions, retail trade will be subject to one code of regulations, wholesale trade to another.

Besides all the health regulations, this kind of business operation will probably be subject to local zoning and licensing laws.

Then there are restrictions on what can and cannot be sold. For example, it is all very well to smoke wild game for personal use, or as gifts to friends, but the *sale* of certain kinds of game meat may be illegal!

Common prudence demands that all such legal points should be checked *before* any commercial operations are undertaken. It would be disastrous to spend a lot of money on equipment, materials and advertising, to enter into contracts for production and sale of smoked foods, and then to be closed down for breach of some law or regulation!

When legal obstacles are overcome, the next problem is to gain customers. For this purpose, nothing beats a taste demonstration.

Some people are prejudiced against smoked foods.

"I've tried smoked turkey; it was so dry I didn't like it!"

"Jerky? That stuff went out with the horse and buggy! Anyway, I know it'd be too tough for my liking."

True, *some* old-fashioned smoking methods did leave foods dry, tough, and rather tasteless except for the smoke flavor. But the proof of the pudding is in the eating. A potential customer cannot argue with his own taste-buds!

A few samples are produced, fresh and succulent, having been wrapped in plastic or aluminum foil; the samples are attractively laid out on a white paper plate (the rich color shows up well that way); the customer is offered a nice white paper napkin to wipe his fingers.

As he nibbles, his objections are temporarily silenced; he has to listen.

"Yes, maybe the smoked jerky that the cowboys used to get was tough enough to sole their boots with. But this salami (or chicken, or shrimp, etc.) isn't just 'smoked'; it's specially seasoned, then cooked in a smoke oven to give it that special smoke flavor, and yet keep it moist and succulent. It's a whole new taste treat!"

Meanwhile the customer is eating, and finds that it's all true!

Once the initial favorable impression is made, development of the business depends upon reliability of production schedules and deliveries, plus consistent quality.

# Appendix

READERS IN SOME AREAS MAY have to do a little detective work to get the equipment and supplies for making certain smoked foods. Home smoking was for some years out of fashion, so there is little or no regular retail trade in the materials required. However, by making some inquiries, one can discover sources of supply. Here are some hints.

## EQUIPMENT

### Ovens

### Smoke Ovens

Portable metal and ceramic ovens are sold in supermarkets, department stores and hardware stores.

### Meat Cutting Tools

Knives, cleavers, steels, hones and saws are sold in hardware stores and department stores.

### Meat Pumps, Meat Grinders, Sausage Stuffers

Consult the Yellow Pages of your phone book, under such headings as Butcher's Equipment & Supplies, Meat Packer's Equipment & Supplies, Restaurant Equipment & Supplies.

## SUPPLIES

### Brine Ingredients, Sausage Seasonings, Sausage Casings

Consult Yellow Pages under the headings mentioned above; also under Sausage Casings.

### Sawdust and Wood Chips

Consult Yellow Pages under Sawdust & Shavings, Wood, Wood Turning, Wood Products, etc. Firms that manufacture hardwood products may be willing to give or sell sawdust and shavings.

Small packages of chips are generally sold at sporting goods stores, hardware stores, and wherever portable smokers are sold.

When I need a great amount of chips, I rent a chipper and make my own from any suitable wood available in the neighborhood. These homemade chips can be stored for years in plastic bags as they are dried before packaging and kept dry afterwards.